I0115568

The *Secret*

CODE TO ABUNDANCE

Understanding God's Secret method for
Prospering His people to Live the days of
Heaven on the Earth

Dr Charles Omole

Author, Breakthrough Strategies for
Christians in the Marketplace

Published by: Winning Faith Outreach Ministries

ISBN: 978-1-907095-23-8

WINNING FAITH
OUTREACH MINISTRIES

London. New York. Boston. Lagos

Published in the United Kingdom.

TABLE OF CONTENTS

INTRODUCTION

Accuracy in the things of God is essential for the manifestation of divine purpose on the earth. That was why God gave Moses and later David some clear and detailed blueprints of the Temples He requested.

For a long time; prosperity in the Kingdom of God has been reduced by the Church to a matter of sowing and reaping alone. At Church service after service we hear of the need to sow financially to be able to reap a financial harvest. While this principle is not wrong; it is grossly incomplete for a believer.

In this book, I will be unveiling what God's "secret' code is to prosper His people in addition to the well understood seed and harvest principle. The seed and harvest mandate was not address to the Church; but to the whole of humanity. That is why if a farmer plants a seed on the ground (regardless of his religion) it will grow. This is a mandate given to all of mankind to exploit the earth's system for increase.

Surely, we as believers cannot be restricted to the same principle that works for everyone else. There must be additional distinguishing factor for a child of God. This was the reason I searched the scriptures to find out God's original intention and plan to proper his people had our first parents not disobeyed God.

So, we as Children of God have additional tool God put in place to distinguish us above all others. I have used the word "secret" in the title of this book with some artistic licence. This is because the secret code is not so secret as you will find out.

As citizens of heaven who occupy the earth; we operate in two realms and have tools that come with each. In this book, I will show you through scriptural precedent and evidence, how you can live above the systems of this world. How you must sow on the earth in order to be able to reap (as an occupier of the earth) and also how as a citizen of heaven, you can overrule the limitations of the earth to prosper.

Yes, we have to operate the principle of financial sowing and reaping like everyone else; but we are not limited to that alone. We can engage God's secret code to produce abundance on the earth. Knowledge of witty inventions. Hidden riches of secret places. These can only be obtained through obedience.

Get ready to be transformed as you renew your mind in the word of God to unleash His abundance over all you do on the earth. I pray this book will encourage your heart and fortify your resolve to live the days of heaven on the earth.

Finally, I have included a **Bonus material section** at the end of this book. This section teaches you how the human spirit, soul and body function as a way to help you learn how to be sensitive to the instructions of God and obey His commands and instructions. I trust this section will bless you richly. At the end, I have provided some blank "Notes" pages for you to document your thoughts and contemplations without the need for a separate notebook.

This may be the best book you have ever read in a long time as I unveil the secret of living above the limitations and systems of the world.

Welcome to Kingdom living. Welcome to a life of Dominion. God bless you bountifully as you seek and obey Him.

With much Blessings, always

Dr Charles Omole
2019

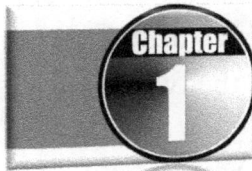

TOUCHING HEAVEN
CHANGING EARTH
Operating in Two Domains

UNDERSTANDING SEEDTIME AND HARVEST

Eden operated like little heaven as God's presence made all things possible and easy for Adam and Eve. But the moment sin came and man was driven out of Eden; it became necessary for TWO systems to evolve as far as humanity was concerned. God's system was operating in the garden; hence His will was done on earth as it was in heaven. But after the fall of mankind; Satan who gained the title deed of the earth started to rig the systems on the earth, creating divergence from the previous unity that existed between the two realms.

So, God decided the earth has to operate based on certain rules which applies to all that live on earth. But as heaven's citizens, we have additional tool only available and operational on the basis of relationship with God through Christ Jesus.

Gen.8:20-22

*[20] Then Noah built an altar to the LORD, and took of every clean animal and of every clean bird, and **offered burnt offerings on the altar**. [21] And the LORD smelled a soothing aroma. Then the LORD said in His heart, "I will never again curse the ground for man's sake, although the imagination of man's heart is evil from his youth; nor will I again destroy every living thing as I have done. [22] "**While the earth remains,***

Seedtime and harvest, Cold and heat, Winter and summer, And day and night Shall not cease."

This is a very popular and familiar passage in the Bible that many in the Church use to explain the need to sow seed in order to reap a harvest. Otherwise called, the principle of Sowing and Reaping.

This is a valid biblical principle, but it is not the complete picture as it relates to God's ways of prospering His followers.

The passage in Genesis 8 quoted above reveal three salient facts we need to understand.

✓ **This is an Earth-Centric Rule.** It says, *"as long as the earth remains".* So, the principle is meant to work only on the earth and for those occupying the earth. This was a rule instituted by God to thrive on the earth by ALL its inhabitants.

✓ **This is a principle in perpetuity.** Seed time and harvest will only cease when there is no longer earth; or cold and heat etc. This is to guarantee the certainty of operation for this principle. *"As long as the earth remains…"* is pretty much a contingent element that makes working this principle infallible in this realm.

✓ **This scripture was not addressed to believers, but to all of Mankind as a whole.** This passage of the Bible was not addressed to Christians, but to ALL occupants of the earth. So, this is not a Christian principle, but a life-principle for all. It is fact that anyone can plant a seed into the ground and it will grow regardless of their faith or no faith at all. Anybody who plants on right soil will see the seed grow. That is why farmers are from all religions and backgrounds. You don't have to be a Christian or a believer for your seed to grow on the earth.

As this scripture apply to ALL inhabitants of the earth, it is pertinent to ask the question:

What is the benefit of being a Christian and serving God if unbelievers have equal access to work this principle just like believers? What is the advantage of serving God, if those that do not serve Him have equal access to benefit from this principle?

These were the questions that made me began studying the scripture to dig deep and uncover the real plan God had for humanity and what is God's secret code to abundance for those who serve Him.

There has to be a distinction between those who serve God and those who do not. He has a covenant of Distinction with us as His children.

So, what was God's plan to make Mankind prosper on the earth if Adam and Eve had not fallen into sin. How would they have flourished on the earth if they had remained in the garden of Eden, faithfully serving God?

If we can understand God's original intentions, plans and strategies, we will know how to unlock unlimited abundance on the earth as God never changes. So, His plan remains effective.

This principle of sowing and reaping works for all who apply its principles. Sadly, the Church has also focused exclusively on sowing and reaping as the only way to prosper on the earth.

A focus on this seed principle is not wrong; it is just incomplete. Since all of humanity have equal access to this seed principle; what distinguishes Believers on the earth? If the only tool we have at our disposal to prosper, is also available to all of humanity; what is the point of serving God in the first place?

But God has a special way reserved for those that serve Him. This special way work on the basis of relationship. It is an exclusive technology that compels the earth to yield to its maker and bring forth for God's children as needed. This technology or secret code is what this book will be discussing.

"For our citizenship is in heaven, from which we also eagerly wait for the Saviour, the Lord Jesus Christ." **Philippians 3:20** (NKJV)

The Bible states that our Citizenship is in heaven. But we also operate on the earth. So, we are able to apply rules from BOTH domains to advance and proper.

To be able to understand the secret code to abundance; you have to first understand how citizens of heaven are supposed to operate on the earth.

You have to know the limitations of earthly tools and when to access the dimension of the spirit needed to overturn the limitations on the earth.

LIVING THE DAYS OF HEAVEN ON THE EARTH

"Thus says the Lord: Learn not the way of the [heathen] nations and be not dismayed at the signs of the heavens, though they are dismayed at them, For the customs and ordinances of the peoples are false, empty, and futile; it is but a tree which one cuts out of the forest [to make for himself a god], the work of the hands of the craftsman with the ax or other tool. They deck [the idol] with silver and with gold; they fasten it with nails and with hammers so it will not fall apart or move around." **Jeremiah 10:2-4** (AMP)

"Listen to the message that God is sending your way house of Israel. Listen most carefully; don't take the godless nations as your models. Don't be impressed by their glamour and glitz no matter how much they are impressed. The religion of this people is nothing but smoke. An idol is nothing but a tree chopped down, then shaped by a woodman's axe. They trim it with a tinsel and balls, use hammer and nails to keep it

upright. It's like a scarecrow in a cabbage patch; it can't talk, dead wood that has to be carried - can't walk. Don't be impressed by such stuff it is useless for either good or evil."
Message Translation

God says don't take the Godless nations as your models. One of the challenges and difficulties in the church today is that we have brought what I call the world's models into the church. The world's marketing techniques and using tools also available to the world without emphasising our Exceptionalism as children of the Most High.

The bible says don't take on their models, because we will begin to see that those who have the human knowledge in trouble; like the "experts" managing the collapsing financial institutions in our economies. The Bible says don't take them as your models.

Remember that the Wiseman saw the Star of Jesus when they were busy focusing on heaven, looking at all the celestial stars. It is foolishness to think that the only way to get latest information is by the Internet and worldly media.

Looking unto heaven will give you access to such profound and new information that even the powerful will fear what you carry. As children and ambassadors of God, we need to learn to connect with home-base and not focus too much on the land of our assignment for instructions and guidance.

"Or else, if you will not let My people go, behold, I will send swarms of flies on you and your servants, on your people and into your houses. The houses of the Egyptians shall be full of swarms of flies, and also the ground on which they stand. And in that day I will set apart the land of Goshen, in which My people dwell, that no swarms of flies shall be there, in order that you may know that I am the LORD in the midst of the land. I will make a difference between My

people and your people. Tomorrow this sign shall be". **Exodus 8:21-23**

The land of Goshen is part of the geographical land of Egypt. Even the swarms knew where not to go. Think about it, they did not just fly where they liked. They knew some areas were not to be visited.

We need to understand that there are different and deeper dimensions of God we need to know. The bible says there is a time and season for everything; winter, summer etc. We have to however understand that this does not restrict God, as all the seasons can come together into one, if God wants it to.

He is sovereign. We need to understand that when God is in operation all the seasons are suspended easily so don't get yourself entangled by limiting yourself to the natural dimension of things. When God shows up He takes over.

It's important to understand that when we live the days of Heaven on earth then the laws of earth will be subject to the happenings in Heaven.

To understand this let's go back to the beginning; Genesis 1:1. "In the beginning God created the Heavens and the earth". In the beginning God created the Heaven and the earth; now I will like to ask a couple of key questions:

1) When God created Heaven and Earth in Genesis 1:1, did He create one to be inferior to the other? We know that He created the heavens and the earth but why? Because He wanted two places where He could have fellowship. A place to Fellowship comfortably in Heaven and also comfortably on the earth. As we saw in the Garden of Eden, the bible says God would come in and fellowship with Adam. That was the whole idea.

2) If God created the Heavens and the earth in such a way that one is not inferior to

the other and He created both of them so that He could have fellowship in both, should the standard of living in one be different from the other? For example, the Queen of England; she has Buckingham Palace in London and several other palaces around the country. If you look at Buckingham palace and examine the interior decoration standard; and then look at the other Palaces, you will find that they are of equal standard.

She does not live in the servant-quarters' in Windsor County and then have a big palace in London. All her palaces reflect the level of her wealth and authority. The President of America lives in the White House, but he has a retreat called Camp David. Camp David is not a one bedroom ghetto apartment, while the white house is big and prestigious. Because of who he is, the standard of living in one place is no different from the other.

So, if God created the Heavens and the earth and one is not inferior to the other; then the standard of living in one should not be vastly different from the other, because When God is fellowshipping, He expects the same standard of existence regardless of where He is.

Recently, I read in the media that during a couple's divorce proceedings; the wife was asking for a lot of money. Her argument was how could the children visit their father in a big house and yet return to live with her in a small basement apartment.

Their standard of living must be of comparable standard regardless of which parent they are staying with at any time. Being the legitimate children of their wealthy father, they needed to maintain the same standard of living explained the mother.

In the same way, since God created heaven and earth so that He could have fellowship in both places and we don't doubt the standard in

Heaven; the question is when He comes to earth is He supposed to behave differently because this is a poor cousin of Heaven? ... no, he is supposed to have the comparable standard.

What bothers me is that "if the streets of Heaven are paved with Gold" as many believes literally; how then are we supposed to live here on earth without Gold?   If God is supposed to have fellowship both in Heaven and on earth, then there has to be interactions/exchanges between heaven and earth.

We have reduced Heaven to "my mansion will be bigger than yours"; even though this is not what Heaven is about.   Christ is our advocate, He is not in Heaven right now in charge of a construction project.

We use scriptures that say, "where I am you will be also", "I am on my way to the Father", "In my Father's house there are many mansions, if it were not so I would have told you so" when

Jesus said that He was not on His way to Heaven, He was on His way to the cross.

The important lesson here is God created the Heavens and the Earth. How did He create heaven and earth? By His spoken words.

"by the word of the Lord the Heavens were made and all the host of them by the breadth of His mouth, He gathers the waters of the sea together as a heap He lays up the deep in storehouses, let all the earth fear the Lord, let all the inhabitants of the world stand in awe of Him, for He spoke and it was done He commanded and it stood fast". **Psalm 33:6-9**

"Of old you laid the foundations of the earth and the Heavens are the work of your hand". **Psalm 102: 25**

It's important for you to understand that neither is inferior to the other; both are God's handiwork. If God created both heaven and earth, one cannot be a poor cousin of the other. Hallelujah.

To help you understand this as we go deeper into this discuss, I will show you some interactions between heaven and earth for you to begin to see that both places have God's DNA in them.

Heaven is a place, Heaven is also an experience. But we know that in a court of law, you are not allowed to testify about an event or something you are not a witness to.

Ask yourself as you go around talking to people about Heaven; have you seen Heaven? What interactions have you had with heaven? How authoritative are you in sharing with other people that there is Heaven when you yourself don't know what or where it is?

This is the fundamental of why our witnessing is not as impacting as it should be. Because we are testifying about a place we don't even know much about. If in a natural court of law, hearsay evidence is not admissible then why would it be admissible in the court of the Spirit?

That is why spiritually speaking, you need to be an eyewitness to give effective evidence of what you have witnessed; which is why the bible says we can have the days of heaven here on earth.

When we look at some of the interactions between heaven and earth in the coming chapters; this thesis will become clearer.

In the Bible, we see that people spoke on earth and God heard in Heaven and God spoke in Heaven and people heard on earth.

The question is "where is Heaven"? It's important for you to understand that Heaven is a place but is also an experience. The same with hell, you can be in hell before you get to Hell.

You need to understand that if you have not had an experience of heaven on earth, you cannot be an effective witness of heaven on earth. Hallelujah.

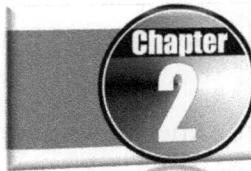

THE SPIRITUAL CONTROL THE PHYSICAL

The standard of living of God's family in Heaven and earth should never be different. We are on earth as heaven's ambassadors. Everything that truly exists in the natural should be a physical manifestation of what already exists in the spirit if it is to last.

The bible says, *"thy will be done on earth as it is in heaven"*. In other words, what is happening on earth is already happened in Heaven. For instance, the bible talks about the Ark of God in Heaven, the temple and tabernacle of God in Heaven, even earthquakes in Heaven; nothing happens here on earth that does not have its existence rooted in the Spirit.

Whatever you are experiencing, or whatever you have here on earth that is not a physical model of what exists in Heaven is not supposed to be your portion. So, if they say you have cancer; is there cancer in Heaven? If the answer is no, then it means you are not supposed to have it.

The Bible says whatever can be seen is temporary and subject to change, but whatever cannot be seen is eternal. This means if the entire basis for the existence of something is earthly with no root in the spirit; then it is temporary and subject to change. But if it is a physical manifestation of a spiritual (unseen) reality; then it is eternal and yours for keeps.

It means the cancer does not have a spiritual root of existence. Its root is limited to the earth.

Hence you can stand and declare that cancer should go because it does not exist where it matters. It will have no choice but disappear. Also, that is why *"the blessing of the Lord maketh rich and it adds no sorrow to it"*, because the root of the blessing is in Heaven.

The bible also talks about "laying treasures for yourself in Heaven" so that whatever happens on earth, depression, inflation or famine, does not affect you financially because your source is in Heaven and as long as the root source is not changing then your physical experience should not change.

But whatever you have physically that is not a reproduction of what exists in Heaven then you can get rid of it. Hallelujah.

Living a life of dominion means living here on earth based on the experiences, the privileges and the resources in Heaven. Understanding this will make you earth-proof in your experiences. Whatever does not exist in Heaven should not exist in you right now. It means before you get to Heaven (the Place), you are already experiencing it. Praise God.

"And it shall come to pass that if ye shall hearken diligently unto my commandments which I command you this day, to love the Lord your God, and to serve him with all your heart and with all your soul; then I will give you the rain for your land in its season, the first rain and the latter rain, that thou mayest gather in thy corn, and thy wine and thine oil. And I will send grass in your fields for your livestock that you may eat and be filled. Take heed to yourself lest your heart be deceived and you turn aside and serve other gods and worship them, lest the Lord's anger be aroused against you and He shut up the Heavens so there will be no rain and the land yield not her products and you perish quickly from the good land which the Lord has given you. Therefore shall ye lay up these my words of mine in your heart and in your soul, and bind them as a sign upon your hand that they may be as frontlets between your eyes. You shall

teach them to your children speaking of them when you sit in your house, when you walk by the way, when you lie down and when you rise up and you shall write them on the doors of the post of your house and on your gates, that your days and days of your children may be multiplied in the land which the Lord swore to your fathers to give them as the days of Heaven upon the earth". **Deuteronomy 11:13-21**

This scripture talks about the longevity and quality of our earthly experience; being comparable to that in heaven. In other words; you live here on earth with the resources of Heaven, above the earthly system, as citizens of Heaven.

The Bible says we are a stranger in a strange land. We are not supposed to conform to the ways of the world and that is why the Bible says, "even though we are in the world, we are not of the world".

"I am a stranger and a temporary resident on the earth; hide not Your commandments from me." **Psalm 119:19**

We as believers, are not supposed to live according to their standards in the world; don't copy them; don't model yourselves after the heathen cities because we are supposed to live in dominion on earth.

Our experience is supposed to be different. What was said in verse 21 of Deuteronomy 11 was repeated in psalm 89, because we need more than one witness.

From verse 11 of psalm 89 the bible says *"the Heavens are yours and the earth also is yours; as for the world and the fullness thereof thou has founded them".*

"But my faithfulness and my mercy shall be with him and in my name his horn shall be exalted". Also I will set his hand over the sea and his right hand over the rivers he shall cry to me you are

my father, my God and the rock of my salvation. Also I will make him my firstborn, higher than the kings of the earth. My mercy will I keep for him for evermore and my covenant shall stand fast with him". His seed also will I make to endure forever and his throne as the days of Heaven". **Verses 24-29**

God has his families both in Heaven and on earth so both places have to be able to reflect a standard worthy of God's reputation.

"now therefore you are no longer strangers and foreigners, but fellow citizens with the saints and members of the household of God: having been built upon the foundation of the apostles and prophets, Jesus Christ himself being the chief corner stone"; in whom the whole building being fitted together grow into a holy temple in the Lord, in whom ye also are builded together for an habitation of God through the Spirit. **Ephesians 2:19-21**

"For this reason I bow my knees to the father of our Lord Jesus Christ, from whom the whole family in Heaven and earth is named". So God has families in both places. From verse 16; "He will grant you according to the riches of His glory to be strengthened with might by His Spirit in the inner man; that Christ may dwell in your hearts by faith; that ye, being rooted and grounded in love may be able to comprehend with all saints what is the breadth, and length and depth and height, and to know the love of Christ which passeth knowledge that ye might be filled with all the fullness of God" **Ephesians 3:14-16**

You need to understand that you have connections to both Heaven and earth whilst still living. You are not just an earthly being or purely just a Heavenly being otherwise you would not have a physical body. You are supposed to be connecting with Heaven while you are here on earth.

First Corinthians Chapter 15 verse 49: *"As we are born the image of the earthly man so shall also be that we shall also bear the image of the Heavenly man."*

The new Living translation of 1Corinthians Chapter 15 verse 49 says *"just as we are now like the earthly man we will some day be like the Heavenly man"*. As it is in Heaven so it is on earth. Hallelujah.

"Then the temple of God was opened in heaven, and the ark of His covenant was seen in His temple. And there were lightnings, noises, thunderings, an earthquake, and great hail". **Revelations 11:19**

These things exists here on earth because it also exists in Heaven.

"After these things I looked and behold the temple of the tabernacle of the testimony in Heaven was opened; and the seven angels came out of the temple, having the seven plagues

clothed in pure and white linen and having their breasts girded with golden girdles. And one of the four beasts gave unto the seven angels seven golden vials full of the wrath of God, who liveth for ever and ever. And the temple was filled with smoke from the glory of God and from His power; and no man was able to enter into the temple, till the seven plagues of the seven angels were fulfilled". **Rev. 15:5-8**

When everything was done and the temple was ready it was filled with smoke representing the glory of the Lord. And the bible says no man was able to enter. But also on earth; that is the same thing that happened, if you look at Exodus Chapter 40, when the tabernacle was completed.

Verse 34 says *"then a cloud covered the tent of the congregation, and the glory of the Lord filled the tabernacle and Moses was not able to enter the tabernacle because the cloud abode thereon and the glory of the Lord filled the tabernacle"*.

As it is in Heaven so it is on earth.

When a permanent temple was later erected to God in Jerusalem listen to what happened. When this new completed temple had the Ark of God moved into it. First King Chapter 8 verse 10-11 says: *"and it came to pass when the priests were come out of the holy place, that the cloud filled the house of the Lord. So that the priests could not stand to minister because of the cloud; for the glory of the Lord had filled the house of the Lord".*

As it is in Heaven so it is on earth. God wants to feel at home both in Heaven and on earth – that's why the earth is modelling the things in Heaven, so that God can just show up and feel at home.

There are some stores in the West, like Costco, IKEA etc that are all over the world. They try to arrange their stores in the same way.

In such a way that it does not matter which branch you visit, you don't spend long time trying to find out where items are, as you immediately know where to go because they have designed it identically to the local store you visit regularly.

God wants to just show up on earth and feel at home exactly as He feels in Heaven. That is God's agenda.

SO, WHERE IS HEAVEN

The question here is this: Where is Heaven? How do you become a witness of it? What does it mean to be in Heaven? Lots of Christians say things like "when we get to Heaven…" and I am wondering to myself that if we are supposed to live the days of Heaven on earth; I am not waiting till I get to Heaven I want to live its quality of life while I am still here, in such a way that when I get to Heaven; I will feel at home instantly.

If you think about it, people say the streets of heaven are paved with gold. In that case, some people will not be able to walk in heaven.

Because you have lived with so much poverty mentality here on earth, that if you are taking it literally that the streets are paved with gold you won't be able to walk on it. The whole idea of Heaven and earth is so that God feels at home on earth the same way He feels at home in Heaven; same with you.

God is preparing you, that's why He says you and I can live in dominion here on earth. What stops us from enjoying the days of Heaven here on earth is our ignorance, absolutely it is our ignorance.

My prayer is that by the time you finish this book, you will understand that living an average life on earth is not a good representation of Heaven. You need to begin to question yourself if the way you are living is the way you would be living if you were in Heaven.

If the answer is no, then you need to understand that it is your right to live the days of Heaven on earth. Your story must change.

"If I have told you earthly things, and ye believe not, how shall ye believe, if I tell you of heavenly things? And no man hath ascended up to heaven, but he that came down from heaven, even the Son of man which is in heaven". **John 3:12-13 (KJV)**

Who is speaking here? Jesus of course. Where was he when he was speaking? On earth. But He said that the person speaking is the son of man who has come from

Heaven and who is in heaven. But we know that He was physically on earth when He was speaking. How do you reconcile this? This is what I mean by living a life of dominion.

Jesus was physically here on earth but He knew He was permanently connected to Heaven. And because He was permanently connected to Heaven, He was from Heaven and He is in Heaven.

Even though physically, He was here on earth. Why did He say *"Son of man ..... in Heaven"* because *"not my will but your will be done".* Whatever the father says that's what happens. For you and I what does it mean to be in Heaven? How do we experience it?

You need to understand that even though we are physical human beings we are supposed to be spiritually tuned to the things of the spirit. You need to have your spiritual ears and eyes open so that you begin to see things the way Heaven sees it, so that when you look at things on earth, you will see things completely different from others and people will wonder why? Because you are seeing what others don't see.

"After these things I looked and behold a door was opened in Heaven: and the first voice which I heard was as it were, of a trumpet talking with me which said, come up hither and I will shew thee things which must be hereafter. Immediately I was in the spirit and behold a throne was set in Heaven, and one sat on the

throne, and He that sat was to look upon like a Jasper and a sardine stone and there was a rainbow round about the throne, in sight like unto an emerald". **Revelations 4: 1-3**

John was physically on earth when he had this experience, so in other words being in the spirit is being in Heaven as you are in a state of connection to heaven from earth. Being in the Spirit is being in Heaven. What happened to John was that he was physically here on earth and he got caught up, just like Paul was caught up in the third Heavens.

Living the days of Heaven on earth is you being physically here on earth but being connected to the spirit. This is a requirement for dominion living.

It means you can be sitting or standing, but your spirit man connects to Heaven and as a result you download everything God wants to say, you come back to reality and you know you have been to Heaven. That is what it means.

You come back to yourself and you begin to make decisions that others think are stupid, but you have heard from Heaven. You begin to go in the direction people think you should not go because you have heard from Heaven and ultimately you will be vindicated.

So, to step into the spirit is to bring Heaven to earth. Consequently, whatever has not been settled in the spirit cannot be manifested in the natural in an enduring way. So, it's important that you understand that stepping into the spirit is what it means to be in Heaven, while on earth. And that is the experience many Christians don't have.

Glimpses of Heaven is not new and there are books that have been written by people that God has taken into the spirit to show different things. I remember, one book written over a decade ago called "Ministry of Angels".

The authors said that when they had the angelic encounter; they had a burning question in their mind to ask. And that was "how did the wall of Jericho collapse given how thick the wall was"?

Although the children of Israel were so close to the wall yet were not crushed. And they recorded in the book the angel said "we used our hands to pushed the wall down from the top".

When connected to heaven, you will begin to hear things that normally you won't hear. It's like a TV signals and radio waves. They exist but unless you have the equipment you can live as if it does not exist.

When we live the days of Heaven on earth, it's about us sharpening our spiritual equipment so that even though we are here, physically and naturally; we are also connected to the heavenly realm.

You are already receiving from Heaven; you are downloading from Heaven; that is what it means.

This way you begin to experience natural things supernaturally and supernatural things naturally. But the difficulty is that many of us when we are in difficulty we would have focused on human methods first before we even remember God.

Many of us tend to go back to God after all the physical buttons we have pressed have not worked.

There are certain battles you cannot fight in your own strength, it's not possible. You need to know where to go and you need to fine-tune the equipment that tunes up to that frequency so that when everyone will be panicking and you will just be calm and smiling.

Whatever there is on earth that is not a reproduction of Heaven's version is temporal and can be changed. I need you as we end this chapter, to begin to look at your life, everything that exists that is not a replica of Heaven is temporal and is subject to change.

So, diseases will die and lack will vanish. Your life is about to enter a new level in God. I am excited for you. You are blessed.

Therefore, with the foregoing understanding, I hope you now appreciate that we should be operating under a HIGHER LAW. Seedtime and harvest is available for us to use as occupiers of the earth; but we are not limited to that pathway alone to prosper on the earth.

As citizens of heaven we can bring additional resources to bear on the earth (since the spiritual controls the physical) in our journey to abundance.

"While the earth remains………

But are we as Believers limited to only earthly resources?

"Blessed be the God and Father of our Lord Jesus Christ, who has blessed us with every

*spiritual **blessing in the <u>heavenly places</u>** in Christ"*. **Eph 1:3**

No, we are not limited to earthly resources alone.

*[3] Blessed be the God and Father of our Lord Jesus Christ, who according to His great mercy has caused us to be born again to a living hope through the resurrection of Jesus Christ from the dead, [4] to obtain an **inheritance which is imperishable and undefiled and will not fade away, reserved in heaven for you.*** **1 Peter 1:3-4** (NASB)

If you can access the blessing in heavenly places; then you can enforce your supply through heavenly resources.

If the resources of the earth are contingent on SEEDTIME and HARVEST; the Bible did not say that resources of heaven work on the same principle. We have camped around seedtime and harvest alone for too long in the Church; when in fact God has additionally created a secret pathway for His children.

Chapter 3

UNDERSTANDING GOD'S SECRET CODE

As previously explained; seedtime and harvest is not only limited to the earthly realm but also available to all of humanity not just Believers.

So, what happens when seedtime and harvest seem to stop working? You have been sowing but there appears to be no harvest. What do you do?

Satan as the ruler of the darkness of this world controls a lot of what happens on earth. So God had to create an additional pathway to abundance that works only on the basis of relationship with Him as the King of all kings. This additional pathway is what I have called the "secret code"; (with some artistic license). The abundance is still resident here on the earth; but access to them will be by God's secret code. Divine guidance is the key to divine prominence.

We are citizens of heaven operating on the earth. So, we have additional tools which sadly most Believers fail to utilise. Some due to ignorance, but others through unbelief.

We were warned in the Bible not to lay treasures up for ourselves on the earth. This is because whatever is on earth; falls within the control of the enemy.

Consequently therefore, BOTH our seed and harvest on the earth are within the reach of the enemy. He can access your seed as well as your harvest, as long as they are on the earth.

"Do not lay up for yourselves treasures on earth, where moth and rust destroy and where thieves break in and steal; 20 but lay up for yourselves treasures in heaven, where neither moth nor rust destroys and where thieves do not break in and steal." **Matthew 6:19-20** (NKJV)

But the Bible states that our citizenship is in heaven. This confers on us certain rights and privileges that are inaccessible to those who are only earth citizens (those not saved).

"For our citizenship is in heaven, from which we also eagerly wait for the Savior, the Lord Jesus Christ." **Phil.3:20**

"And as we have borne the image of the earthly man, we shall also bear[a] the image of the heavenly Man." **1 Corinthians 15:49**

If it is seed that gives you harvest on the earth; what gives you access to resources in the heavenly places? It cannot be the same thing otherwise there is no difference between heaven and earth.

*"First, I thank my God through Jesus Christ for you all, that your faith is spoken of throughout the whole world. For God is my witness, whom I serve with my spirit in the gospel of His Son, that without ceasing I make mention of you always in my prayers, making request if, by some means, now at last I may find a way in the will of God to come to you. **For I long to see you, that I may impart to you <u>some</u> spiritual <u>gift,</u> so that you may be established**— that is, that I may be encouraged together with you by the mutual faith both of you and me.* **Rom.1:8-12**

In these verses of scripture, *"Spiritual Gift"* is singular; so, the use of "some" before it looks out of place. *'Some'* usually go with something that is more than one. Like *"some cars", "some houses"* etc. *"Some car"* is bad English tense construction.

So, when the Bible says *"...Some spiritual gift..."* we need to check its true meaning and context.

"Some" here means UNFAMILIAR (e.g *Some Man is here to see you*...by the Secretary to her Boss).

Paul is saying I am coming to impart unto you the gift you are 'not familiar with'...*so that they will be established in new truth.*

"O you afflicted one, Tossed with tempest, and not comforted, Behold, I will lay your stones with colorful gems, And lay your foundations with sapphires. [12] I will make your pinnacles of rubies, Your gates of crystal, And all your walls of precious stones. [13] All your children shall be taught by the LORD, And great shall be the peace of your children. [14] In righteousness you shall be established; You shall be far from oppression, for you shall not fear; And from terror, for it shall not come near you.

[15] Indeed they shall surely assemble, but not because of Me. Whoever assembles against you shall fall for your sake. **Isa.54:11-15**

These verses are vivid reflections of the financial state of many Believers. It is like tempest. Have today and lack tomorrow. You oscillate between abject need and some supply. This is not God's plan for His children.

In Romans 1:8-12 that was quoted previously, Apostle Paul is saying in addition to your FAITH; you still need spiritual GIFT impartation before you can be established in God and increase.

*"For I long to see you, that I may impart to you **some spiritual gift**, so that you may be established."*

What is the "some" GIFT that Paul refers?
*"In **righteousness you shall be established**; You shall be far from oppression [Pressure], for you*

shall not fear; And from terror, for it shall not come near you. **Isaiah 54:14 - (NKJV)**

So, (putting together Romans 1 and Isaiah 54) if 'Some Spiritual Gift ESTABLISHES us'…. And … 'Righteousness also ESTABLISHES us'… Then the two must be linked. There must be a connection between 'some spiritual GIFT' and 'righteousness'.

This "unfamiliar (some) Gift" that Apostle Paul refers is access to the supernatural realm so that they are not just limited to what the earth has to offer. The Roman Church had not yet been exposed to the Apostolic grace that Paul carried and they needed it to be established.

The Roman Christians had not yet received any of these miraculous endowments, and thus they differed widely from all the other Churches which had been raised by the apostle's ministry. From this it appears that he desired to be among them to exercise the office of the ministry, to establish them in the gospel and to confirm their hopes.

HOW DO YOU ACCESS THIS SUPERNATURAL SUPPLY REALM?

"For I long to see you, that I may impart to you some spiritual gift, so that you may be established." **Rom.1**[11]

"...that is, that I may be encouraged together with you by the mutual faith both of you and me." **Rom.1** [12]

It takes the mutual faith of both you (your faith) and me (my grace) to gain access to this realm of supernatural supply. This will be same for any other prophet of God carrying this grace for abundance. There are certain dimensions of the supernatural that only an Apostolic grace can open for the Church.

Paul is saying I know of your great faith, but you still need the grace that I carry (Apostolic grace) to add to your faith to get you established. In this book, I have brought you the grace that command resources today. Will you stretch your faith to connect with it? I pray that you receive this today in Jesus mighty name.

It was a wish of benevolence, and accords with what Paul said concerning his intended visit in **Romans 15:29** when he declared: *"And I am sure that when I come, I shall come in the fullness of the blessing of the gospel of Christ."*

To make known to them more fully the blessings of the gospel, and thus to impart 'some spiritual gift', was the purpose he had in mind. There is certain empowerment that only Apostles can convey on the Church. In his commentary on the New Testament, Coffman said concerning these verses as follows:

> "The particular spiritual gift Paul had in mind was not mentioned, and it is pointless to speculate; but one sure conclusion that seems justified from this

verse is that no apostle had ever been in Rome at the time this letter was sent; otherwise, the intended spiritual gift would already have been conveyed.

Romans 1:12 was written from considerations of tact. Paul, not wishing to appear as high and mighty above the band of believers in Rome, did not speak merely of his conferring some benefit upon them, but also of the mutual benefit in which he himself would also share. The use of the words "that is" indicates that Paul, after writing the preceding words, sought to soften their impact by mention of the blessing he himself would receive from them. The delicacy, understanding, and humility of this great Christian apostle stand out conspicuously in this warm, personal passage."

So, we know Apostle Paul carried an apostolic grace needed to unlock a dimension of empowerment over the Church in Rome. This is not any extraordinary gift of the Spirit; but spiritual light, knowledge, peace, and comfort, through the exercise of his ministerial gift. This is still the case today. Every Church need the Apostolic grace to unfold to them dimensions of the spirit they are unfamiliar with.

Once this grace is unleashed, then there are certain outputs or manifestations that should be evident in the lives of such Believers.

*"Now I do not want you to be unaware, brethren, that I often planned to come to you (but was hindered until now), that I might have **some fruit** among you also, just as among the other Gentiles. [14] I am a debtor both to Greeks and to barbarians, both to wise and to unwise. [15] So, as much as is in me, I am ready to preach the gospel to you who are in Rome also."* **Romans 1[13]**

You can see here again the word 'some' being used with a singular "fruit". This means the same as in Romans. This "some fruit" means fruits they are unfamiliar with; that they have not manifested before now.

So, 'some gift' will produce 'some fruit'.
What is it that Paul was bringing to them: *'Some Gift'*
What is it that Paul wants from them: *Some Fruit.*

What the Apostle was saying is that, I carry a grace that unfolds to you a dimension of knowledge and spiritual light; that when activated in righteousness will produce "Some Fruit" in them.

It is this "some fruit" that Believers will need to access our supply in heavenly places as citizens of heaven.

While harvest and supply on the earth is a function of your SEED; you cannot access heavenly places with earthly seed. Otherwise every unbeliever will have access to heaven by simply sowing.

Supply from Heaven is a function of our FRUIT not our earthly SEED. As citizens who come from one realm but operates in another; we have been given the capacity to exploit BOTH realms to the glory of God.

We sow seed to get harvest as the earth's rules demand; but as the enemy have access to both earthly seed and harvest; God has kept additional resources for us in Heavenly places, but can only be accessed by our FRUIT so to speak. This is the dimension of grace that Apostle Paul said the Roman Church was "Unfamiliar" with.

THEREFORE:
It takes FRUIT to access the things that are in heaven not SEED. On the Earth; you need SEED to access Harvest. But in Heaven *(Heavenly Places);* you need FRUIT to access Supernatural Supply.

SEED is not the same as FRUIT. The Confusion over this has been the cause of lack in many lives of the Saints of God; who have been restricted to only earthly seed and harvest in their quest to access Kingdom wealth.

Access to Supernatural Supply Realm in heaven is via FRUITS and not via SEED. *Seed is limited to the earthly realm. FRUIT relates to the things that are in heaven.*

"Blessed be the God and Father of our Lord Jesus Christ, who has blessed us with every spiritual blessing in the heavenly places in Christ." **Ephesians 1:3**

Why will God put the blessings in heavenly places when the beneficiaries are here on the earth? As stated in the previous Chapter, this because we are supposed to be able to access heavenly places from the earth.

When you sow your SEED you are connecting to the earth, but when you live in Righteousness and manifest your FRUIT you are connecting to Heaven.

So, to summarise:

- ✓ How do you access the harvests on the Earth; by sowing SEED.
- ✓ How do you access the things that are heavenly; by having FRUIT.

¹⁷ Therefore I have reason to glory in Christ Jesus in the things which pertain to God. ¹⁸ For I will not dare to speak of any of those things which Christ has not accomplished through me, in word and deed, to make the Gentiles obedient— ¹⁹ in mighty signs and wonders, by the power of the Spirit of God, so that from Jerusalem and round about to Illyricum I have fully preached the gospel of Christ. ²⁰ And so I have made it my aim to preach the gospel, not where Christ was named, lest I should build on another man's foundation, ²¹ but as it is written: "To whom He was not announced, they shall see; And those who have not heard shall understand."

²² For this reason I also have been much hindered from coming to you. ²³ But now no *longer having a place in these parts, and having a great desire these many years to come to you, [24] whenever I journey to Spain, I shall come to you.[i] For I hope to see you on my journey, and to be helped on my way there by you, if first I may enjoy your company for a while. [25] But now I am going to Jerusalem to minister to the saints. [26] For it pleased those from Macedonia and Achaia to make a **certain contribution** for the poor among the saints who are in Jerusalem. [27] It pleased them indeed, and they are their debtors. For if the Gentiles have been partakers of their spiritual things, their duty is also to minister to them in material things. [28] Therefore, when I have performed this and have sealed to them THIS FRUIT, I shall go by way of you to Spain. [29] But I know that when I come to you, I shall come in the fullness of the blessing of the gospel[i] of Christ.* **Romans 15:17-29**

Carriers of Apostolic anointing can deliberately transmit this race to a person, a people, a church or a community. So, what is this fruit we have been reading about?

"Moreover, brethren, we make known to you the **grace of God** *bestowed on the churches of Macedonia: ² that in a great trial of affliction the abundance of their joy and their deep poverty abounded in the riches of their liberality. ³ For I bear witness that according to their ability, yes, and beyond their ability, they were freely willing,⁴ imploring us with much urgency that we would receive[a] the gift and the fellowship of the ministering to the saints. ⁵ And not only as we had hoped, but they <u>first gave themselves to the Lord, and then to us by the will of God</u> . ⁶ So we urged Titus, that as he had begun, so he would also* **complete this grace** *in you as well. ⁷ But as you abound in everything—in faith, in speech, in knowledge, in all diligence, and in your love for us—see* **that you abound in this grace also.** **2Cor 8:1-7**

Struggle for wealth will stop when you operate in this Grace.

*"But this I say: He who sows sparingly will also reap sparingly, and he who sows bountifully will also reap bountifully. [7] So let each one give as he purposes in his heart, not grudgingly or of necessity; for God loves a cheerful giver. [8] And God is able to **make all grace abound toward you**, that you, **always having** all sufficiency in all things, may have an abundance for every good work. [9] As it is written:*

He has dispersed abroad, He has given to the poor; His righteousness endures forever."
*[10] Now may[c] He who supplies **SEED** to the sower, and bread for food, supply and multiply the **seed** you have sown and increase the **FRUITS of your righteousness**, [11] while you are enriched in everything for all liberality, which causes thanksgiving through us to God."*
2Cor.9:6-11

Fruit of your Righteousness is your access to Heaven's resources.

"But I rejoiced in the Lord greatly that now at last your care for me has flourished again;

though you surely did care, but you lacked opportunity. [11] Not that I speak in regard to need, for I have learned in whatever state I am, to be content: [12] I know how to be abased, and I know how to abound. Everywhere and in all things I have learned both to be full and to be hungry, both to abound and to suffer need. [13] I can do all things through Christ[b] who strengthens me.
*[14] Nevertheless you have done well that you shared in my distress. [15] Now you Philippians know also that in the beginning of the gospel, when I departed from Macedonia, no church shared with me concerning giving and receiving but you only. [16] For even in Thessalonica you sent aid once and again for my necessities. [17] **Not that I seek the gift, but I seek <u>THE FRUIT</u> that abounds to your account.** Indeed I have all and abound. I am full, having received from Epaphroditus the things sent from you, **a sweet-smelling aroma** [just like Noah in Gen 8], an acceptable sacrifice, well pleasing to God. [19] And my God shall supply all your need according to His riches in glory by Christ*

Jesus. [20] *Now to our God and Father be glory forever and ever. Amen."* **Phil 4:10-20**

FRUIT is what gives you access to heaven's resources. What FRUIT was Paul seeking?

WHAT IS THIS FRUIT?
The Fruit is not money or about money. The fruit (that is enveloped in Righteousness) has <u>three main dimensions</u> to its manifestation, although the fruit is only ONE thing:

What God requires will depend on each situation. But Righteousness is the container of the FRUIT. When you seek God, making Him your priority and consumed by love for His majesty and living a life of total submission; you will manifest the fruit needed to access heavenly places.

1) The Fruit needed to access what heaven has for you is your **OBEDIENCE** (*as with Abraham when told to sacrifice Isaac*)

i) The Fruit can manifest as your **Sacrificial Love** that provokes heaven's response (*As with Solomon who through his love for God gave a Thousand burnt offerings that provoked heaven's response*).

ii) The Fruit also manifest as **HOLINESS AND GODLY LIVING** that gives you access to His presence (*as with Joseph who lived to please God*). The bible never said Joseph gave (or sowed) any particular offering to God. But his lifestyle of obedience to the will of God was the offering that honoured God and commanded His presence.

The Fruit is OBEDIENCE; but this can be manifested as simple obedience to an instruction or as sacrificial love for God or Godly lifestyle which refuses compromise.

The abundance are situated here on the earth. It is access to them that obedience leads you to.

Satan has rigged the world system to favour those that serve him. So, God through His 'secret code' reverses that advantage. As long as we obey God; we shall eat the good of the land.

The Fruit of Righteousness is what accesses heaven, not your earthly seed. This means; you cannot sow material seed to receive heaven's harvest the way you do on earth. You will need the Fruit of Obedience to access Heaven's hidden riches. Seedtime and harvest only apply to the earth realm and available to ALL of humanity.

Hence, you cannot be an earthly seed sower, but live in disobedience, embracing iniquity and expect to access heavenly places.

You will not have the FRUIT of Righteousness to do so. Mind you; your earthly seed will still produce harvest; but **God's secret code can only be accessed through the FRUIT of righteousness.**

For those operating in the Marketplace, divine guidance and obedience to it is very critical to access the hidden riches of secret places.

*"And I will give thee the treasures of darkness, and **hidden riches of secret places**, that thou mayest know that I, the LORD, which call thee by thy name, am the God of Israel."* **Isaiah 45:3**

These riches are HIDDEN and hidden in SECRET places. That is a double lock that makes access to these riches impossible without God's secret code. Obedience to God's instructions is what leads you to the secret places.

The day you fully get this revelation; you will discover the place called JEHOVAH JIRAH - The place where your obedience commands divine provision. You will begin to spend from the pocket of Jehovah.

As you release your FRUIT; you will access the dimension of the spirit that will command heaven's resources your way.

"There is one who scatters, yet increases more; And there is one who withholds more than is right, But it leads to poverty. ²⁵ ***The generous soul will be made rich,*** *And he who waters will also be watered himself. ²⁶ The people will curse him who withholds grain, But blessing will be on the head of him who sells it. ²⁷ He who earnestly seeks good finds favour, But trouble will come to him who seeks evil.²⁸ He who trusts in his riches will fall, But the righteous will flourish like foliage.*
²⁹ He who troubles his own house will inherit the wind, And the fool will be servant to the wise of heart. ³⁰ ***The FRUIT OF THE RIGHTEOUS is a tree of life,*** *And he who wins souls is wise.* **Prov. 11:24 - 30**

First you get Born Again and gain access into the Kingdom of God. Then you begin to allow the Righteousness of God in you to take over all you do. Then you will begin to bear fruit of righteousness. As you release your FRUIT; you become a TREE of LIFE.

Unlimited supply, Unlimited Grace, Unlimited Abundance, Unlimited Harvest. Glory to God.

*[16] You did not choose Me, but I chose you and appointed you that you should go **and bear fruit, and that your fruit should remain**, that whatever you ask the Father in My name He may give you. John **15:16** - (NKJV)*

It is the Fruit of your Righteousness that access Heaven; not just your earthly seed. A life of total Obedience to God become a Fruit of your Righteousness, which in turn gives you access to heaven's resources.

So;

- ➢ You MUST still sow your SEED to access Harvest on earth
- ➢ And sow your FRUIT to access heaven's reserve for you.

SO, YOU DO BOTH. But you are not LIMITED to just the Earthly resources any longer. You take advantage of Both realms.

The enemy have access to your earthly harvest; but not to your heaven's reserve. Your harvest on earth can be interfered with and wasted by weather conditions, because you live in a fallen world.

Therefore, FRUITFULNESS must precede Supernatural Increase.

The First thing God required of <u>Adam</u> was to be…. FRUITFUL. *(this is not about children because he later said, multiply…)*

FRUITFULNESS in Righteousness is a connector between heaven and earth.

Then to <u>Noah</u>, God also said:
*"So God blessed Noah and his sons, and said to them: "**Be fruitful** and multiply, and fill the earth."* **Gen. 9:1**

Let's look at <u>ISAAC</u>:

*There was a famine in the land, besides the first famine that was in the days of Abraham. And Isaac went to Abimelech king of the Philistines, in Gerar……… **Then Isaac sowed in <u>that land</u>,** and reaped in the same year a hundredfold; and the LORD blessed him. [13] The man began to prosper, and continued prospering until he became very prosperous;…for he had possessions of **flocks** and possessions of **herds** and a **great number of servants**. So the Philistines envied him.* **Gen. 26 1, 12, 14**

This is a very popular scripture. But the question many do not ask is; what did Isaac sow?

The fundamental law of Genesis states that every seed must produce fruit after its own kind. **So what seed did Isaac sow to be getting increases in…flocks…herds… great number of servants**….*did he sow servants?* What seed could he have sown that will manifest in multiple harvest like this?

What did Isaac Sow?

There was no record of Isaac giving any offering in Gerar. We are not told which Church he attended to give offering. Isaac sowed a fruit, not a seed.

ISAAC SOWED OBEDIENCE. He obeyed God despite the impossible and difficult command God gave him. His Obedience became a fruit for him to access God's supply.

He accessed His heaven's reserve through the fruit of Obedience. He stayed where he was told to stay, despite famine.

He did not allow the bad situation on the ground to make him question or disobey God's command. But who also benefited from this supernatural Grace?

"But the herdsmen of Gerar quarreled with Isaac's herdsmen, saying, "The water is ours." So he called the name of the well Esek,[a] because they quarreled with him. 21 Then

*they dug another well, and they quarreled over that one also. So he called its name Sitnah.[b] 22 And he moved from there and dug another well, and they did not quarrel over it. So he called its name Rehoboth,[c] because he said, "For now the LORD has made **room for us**,[not Me] and we shall be fruitful in the land."* **Gen. 26:20-22**

Why use the multiple 'us'?
Because the Grace that was on Isaac is now benefiting ALL his servants and allies, not just him alone.

May you be rightly connected in the season of famine. You cannot separate supernatural Increase from Fruitfulness.

Isaac's prayer for Jacob:
Genesis 28:3 - (NKJV)
*"May God Almighty bless you, And make you **fruitful** and multiply you, That you may be an assembly of peoples."*

Concerning <u>Joseph</u>:

Genesis 49:22 - [22] *"Joseph is **a fruitful bough, A fruitful bough** by a well; His branches run over the wall"*.

You cannot separate supernatural increase from Fruitfulness. There is a dimension of the fruitfulness that is consequence of their relationships with God.

Just operating by Seedtime and Harvest have limitations on the earth for a child of God. How do I mean? What can happen to your earthly seed and harvest?

1. **Your Harvest is subject to weather & other earthly conditions:**
   If the rain does not fall, your harvest can be affected even though you have sowed your seed. Deut 11: 10-15

*"For the land which you go to possess is not like the land of Egypt from which you have come, where **you sowed your seed** and watered it by*

foot, as a vegetable garden; ¹¹ *but the land which you cross over to possess is a land of hills and valleys, which drinks water from the rain of heaven,* ¹² *a land for which the LORD your God cares; the eyes of the LORD your God are always on it, from the beginning of the year to the very end of the year.*

¹³ *'And it shall be that if you **earnestly OBEY My commandments which I command you today**, to love the LORD your God and serve Him with all your heart and with all your soul,* ¹⁴ *then I will give you the rain for your land in its season, the early rain and the latter rain, that you may gather in your grain, your new wine, and your oil.* ¹⁵ *And I will send grass in your fields for your livestock, that you may eat and be filled."*
Deuteronomy 11:10-15 (NKJV)

2. Invaders can come and steal your harvest. Your hope must not be in earthly seed.

All the variables can come against you on earth. This will destroy your yield on earth even if you are good at sowing seed.

So you have to be able to operate at a level the enemy cannot reach.....*through your Fruit accessing the heavenly places.*

Isaac case explained

"Therefore hear the parable of the sower: [19] *When anyone hears the word of the kingdom, and does not understand it, then the wicked one comes and snatches away what was sown in his heart. This is he who received seed by the wayside.* [20] *But he who received the seed on stony places, this is he who hears the word and immediately receives it with joy;* [21] *yet he has no root in himself, but endures only for a while. For when tribulation or persecution arises because of the word, immediately he stumbles.* [22] *Now he who received seed among the thorns is he who hears the word, and the cares of this world and the deceitfulness of riches choke the word, and he becomes unfruitful.* [23] *But he who received seed on the good ground is he who* **hears the word and**

understands it, <u>who indeed bears fruit</u> and produces: *some a hundredfold, some sixty, some thirty."* **Mat.13:18-23**

When God spoke the word to Isaac, DO NOT GO to Egypt, stay in the land of Gerar; I will be with you. Isaac received the WORD, Understood it.

Isaac sowed that word into his earth and obeyed. **It was this that became FRUIT; that made him FRUITFUL**

*"Now it shall come to pass, if you **diligently obey the voice** of the* LORD *your God, to observe carefully all His commandments which I command you today, that the* LORD *your God will set you high above all nations of the earth.* [2] *And all these blessings shall come upon you and overtake you, because you obey the voice of the* LORD *your God.* Deut 28:1-2

➢ What did Moses Sow
➢ What did Isaac Sow,

> ➤ What did Joseph Sow
> ➤ What did David Sow

It is all about your Fruit; not just about your earthly seed.

WHAT HAPPENS WHEN YOU BECOME FRUITFUL?

1. When you become fruitful, God guarantee that He will restore the wasted years back to you.

"Be glad then, you children of Zion, And rejoice in the LORD *your God; For He has given you the former rain faithfully,*[a] *And He will cause the rain to come down for you— The former rain, And the latter rain in the first month.* [24] *The threshing floors shall be full of wheat, And the vats shall overflow with new wine and oil.* [25] *"So I will restore to you the years that the swarming locust has eaten, The crawling locust, The consuming locust, And the chewing locust,*[b] *My great army which I sent among you.*

You shall eat in plenty and be satisfied, And praise the name of the LORD your God, Who has dealt wondrously with you; And My people shall never be put to shame. ²⁷ *Then you shall know that I am in the midst of Israel: I am the LORD your God And there is no other. My people shall never be put to shame.*
Joel 2:23-27

2. When you become fruitful, you become a forbidden territory for the Devourer.

Because the source of your increase is not earthly, you become a forbidden space for the enemy to successfully operate. His efforts will no longer yield any outcome in your life. You are unstoppable.

3. Fruitfulness is your unmistakable Identity

Fruitfulness is a key distinguishing factor between those that serve God and those that do not. The secret code works on the basis of relationship. And that is relationship with God through the sacrifice of Christ on the cross.

"Beware of false prophets, who come to you in sheep's clothing, but inwardly they are ravenous wolves. [16] You will know them by their fruits. Do men gather grapes from thorn bushes or figs from thistles? [17] Even so, every good tree bears good fruit, but a bad tree bears bad fruit. [18] A good tree cannot bear bad fruit, nor can a bad tree bear good fruit. [19] Every tree that does not bear good fruit is cut down and thrown into the fire. [20] Therefore by their fruits you will know them. **Mat 7: 15- 20**

"We give thanks to the God and Father of our Lord Jesus Christ, praying always for you, [4] since we heard of your faith in Christ Jesus and of your love for all the saints; [5] because of the hope which is laid up for you in heaven, of which you heard before in the word of the truth of the gospel, [6] which has come to you, as it has also in all the world, **and is bringing forth**

fruit,[a] *as it is also among you since the day you heard and knew the grace of God in truth.....*

[9] *For this reason we also, since the day we heard it, do not cease to pray for you, and to ask that you may be filled with the knowledge of His will in all wisdom and spiritual understanding;* [10] *that you may walk worthy of the Lord, fully pleasing Him,* **being fruitful in every good work** *and increasing in the knowledge of God;* [11] *strengthened with all might, according to His glorious power, for all patience and longsuffering with joy;* [12] *giving thanks to the Father who has qualified us to be partakers of the inheritance of the saints in the light.* [13] *He has delivered us from the power of darkness and conveyed us into the kingdom of the Son of His love,* [14] *in whom we have redemption through His blood,*[b] *the forgiveness of sins.* **Colossians 1:3-14**

There is no supernatural Increase without Fruitfulness

Chapter 4

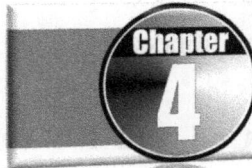

OPERATING THE SECRET CODE FOR INCREASE AND DOMINION

Now that you understand what God's 'secret code' is, how do you operate it on the earth? How do you practically work this divine system?

The three-dimensional manifestation of fruit that command the resources of heaven as explained in the previous Chapter are:
- ✓ Obedience
- ✓ Love for God and
- ✓ Holy & Godly Living.

But if I can some up all three into one word, it will be OBEDIENCE. Loving God is a command and living a life that honours God is also a command. So, doing these things are in fact living in Obedience.

Obedience to God and His commands can therefore be said to be the FRUIT that will grant access to heaven's resources. Everything God created have capacity to obey Him.

So, when there is limitation on earth; when the enemy has taken over your seed or harvest; God knows where the hidden riches are. He will give you command as to what to do. Obedience to His word will unlock the hidden supply.

This message must not be seen as saying you should not sow financial seed. This will be wrong. In fact; sowing financial seed is obeying the commands of God that says we should do so.

Therefore, when you sow financially you are actually walking in obedience too. But your sowing must be divinely directed to be effective. **Divine guidance is the key to operating God's secret code.**

I am also saying Believers additionally have access to heaven's resources to live in plenty. This is not available to those that do not serve the living God.

FOUR PRINCIPLES THAT HELP YOU OPERATE THE SECRET CODE .

To operate in total obedience to God is a process that usually manifest in a particular fashion.

THE FOUR CARDINAL PRINCIPLES

1. YOU MUST HAVE GOD (Relationship): Our relationship with God is key to accessing His secret code.

God created man; then formed him and put him in EDEN (God's Presence). That means the environment Man is supposed to function in is the presence of God. Outside of it; man will Malfunction.

Before Sin; Adam's eyes were opened to the things of the spirit; but blinded to canal things. His relationship with God was the key to his existence.

But after Sin came; the bible says *"their eyes were opened"*. But they were not blind before. So, what happened?

"And when the woman saw that the tree was good for food, and that it was pleasant to the eyes, and a tree to be desired to make one wise, she took of the fruit thereof, and did eat, and gave also unto her husband with her; and he did eat. And the eyes of them both were opened, and they knew that they were naked..." **Gen 3:6-7**

There Spiritual eyes (a function of their relationship with God) was blinded as a result of Sin; but replaced by purely natural eyes. NATURAL EYES CAN ONLY SEE

PHYSICAL THINGS. This is where limitation was born and man could no longer dominate the earth as expected.

The God factor is a re-occurring decimal from Abraham to Isaac, Joseph to Elijah and subsequently Elisha. The obvious reason being that apart from being the creator of the heavens and the earth, He fills them all and knows more about abundant living than anyone else. God know where every hidden thing on earth is. He knows more about this earth than all the scientists put together.

"The earth is the Lord's, and everything in it. The world and all its people belong to him. For he laid the earth's foundation on the seas and built it on the ocean depths." **Psalm 24:1-2 (NLT)**

All provision and blessings flow from Him towards His creation. Thus, relationship with God apart from being the currency of the Spirit remains the connecting conduit between us and our source (God). And He knows where everything is.

"By the God of your father who will help you, And by the Almighty who will bless you With blessings of heaven above, Blessings of the deep that lies beneath, Blessings of the breasts and of the womb." **Genesis 49:25**

Daniel confirms that in Daniel 11:32 when he declared that : "*...but the people who know their God shall be strong, and carry out great exploits.*"

It is wisdom that instructs us to stay connected to the One who has promised that "*They shall not be ashamed in the evil time, And in the days of famine they shall be satisfied.*" (Psalm 37:19).

So, how has your relationship with Him been lately?

God is the Money Magnet. The closer we are to Him; the more we are within His magnetic field.

After all, He owns all things. The farther away we are from Him; the less attracted resources and abundance will be to you. Consider the instructions in Jeremiah 9: 23-24.

"Thus says the Lord: Let not the wise man glory in his wisdom, Let not the mighty man glory in his might, Nor let the rich man glory in his riches; But let him who glories glory in this, That he understands and knows Me, That I am the Lord, exercising lovingkindness, judgment, and righteousness in the earth. For in these I delight," says the Lord.

A relationship with God is the First Step to working and enjoying the secret code to abundance.

2. YOU MUST HAIL GOD (Praise/Worship): While praise brings God into our situation (Psalm 22:3) worship translates us into His very presence and creates room for communion as we behold His face.

The presence of God ensures provision, protection and direction. Worship guarantees the presence of God being manifested. (Gen. 22:9-14, Ex. 13:21-22, Ex. 14:19-20, Ex. 33:14-15, Ps. 16:11).

When we praise God, the earth will yield her increase!

*"Let the peoples praise You, O God; Let all the peoples praise You. **Then** the earth shall yield her increase; God, our own God, shall bless us. God shall bless us, And all the ends of the earth shall fear Him."* **Psalm 67: 5-7**

The place of worship is also the place of prayer; a humbling encounter that brings our humanity under the sovereignty of the Almighty God. (Psalm 61:1-4).

The presence of God builds trust in us and reinforces the needed virtue of waiting and patience within us. (Psalm 40:1-3, Heb. 6:12).

Finally, thanksgiving is an attitude of gratitude that demonstrates our faith, seals our testimony and ensures constant favour before God. So, in all things give Him thanks!

"Rejoice always, pray without ceasing, 18 in everything give thanks; for this is the will of God in Christ Jesus for you." **1Thess. 5:16-18**

So how truthful has our worship and dedication to Him been, John4: 23-24? Has our praise life been qualified or dictated by circumstances, conditions, and feelings. Can we praise Him sacrificially? Habakkuk 3: 17.

David of a truth knew how to prioritize God and it paid off on all fronts. Lord, give me a heart that yearns for you. I need an unquenchable desire to be where you dwell; in your presence oh Lord.

3. YOU MUST HEAR GOD (Communion):
An expected end-result and dividend of worship is communion.

The three major outcomes of divine encounter are illumination, inspiration and revelation. In the midst of global economic depression; divine direction remains a key to moving from survival, to being buoyant and ultimately experiencing abundance.

Our fathers of faith operated under Divine Direction. And it worked for them every time.

- ✓ It ensured Isaac was not derailed in famine (Gen 26:1-14).

- ✓ Joseph under the influence had clear interpretation of Pharaoh's dreams and knew what to do before famine hit the land of Egypt and the rest of the world (Gen. 41:1-36, vs 56).

- ✓ Similarly, Elijah knew where to go in the midst of famine (1kings 17: 9).

- ✓ God's word in the mouth of Elisha produced a major turnaround in Israel during famine. (2Kings 7:1&18)

God's counsel comes in diverse forms-dreams, visions, prophecy, word of knowledge, word of wisdom, small still voice within, His spoken and revealed word (Rhema) and circumstances around us. All these are made possible by the Holy Spirit, God's seal of sonship. (1Cor.2:9-10).

God speaks and He lives! (Gen 41:45, Isaiah 30:21). But is anyone listening? Are you?

As a son and daughter of God, have you heard from your father lately? Have we by compromise, negligence or outright disobedience on the last instructions now miss the privilege of hearing Him? Eli was anointed but became dull of hearing. 1 Samuel 3: 1-4.

Ability to hear is relative to obedience to earlier instructions. Hebrew 5: 11-14, Psalm 25: 14; Genesis 18: 17, 18, 33; Psalm 110:1.

Then finally,

4. YOU MUST HEED HIM (Obedience):
Whenever God speaks, He expects us to hear Him, believe Him and obey Him. This obedience is the fruit that produces abundance, even in the midst of famine. Simply obey God and leave the consequences to Him.

Hearing without heeding can only produce failure and hardship in life not only in periods of famine but at all times... Remember *"...Believe in the LORD your God, and you shall be established; believe His prophets, and you shall prosper."* 2 Chronicles 20:20.

The only proof of belief is obedience! It is obedience that leads you to the hidden riches of the earth. It is obedience that makes God's secrets available to you. Obedience enables you to take on the capability of God as He leads you beside the still waters.

It is absolutely unimaginable what would have become of Isaac, Joseph (and even Pharaoh!),

Elijah and Elisha if they had not obeyed God? Destruction!! (Deut 28:15-68, Isa 1:20).

Obedience is not only the highest form of worship but an act that activates the manifestation of God's promises and His power. This is the basis for releasing His secret code to abundance. Where the voice of the Lord leads; there will always be abundance and sufficiency; (Deut. 28:1-14).

According to Isaiah 1: 19; if we are willing and obedient, we shall eat the good of the land. In these days, as believers, we must translate divine information to action in order to experience God's transforming power and abundance.

The media is full of discouraging facts and conflicting signals. (Isaiah 66:6). However, God's counsel remains the only beacon of hope and comfort in famine. Let us set aside doubts, unbelief, rebellion, strife and covetousness and embrace obedience as an enduring lifestyle.

The 'sermon on the mount' is lived out in the midst of men after descent. Global famine is already here with us. God has not only warned us about famine but has prepared and made provision for us to flourish in famine.

Establishing covenant relationship with God by the blood of Jesus Christ is the connecting point. Worship and Communion reinforce the relationship by ensuring constant flow of heart-to-heart communication with the father.

Obedience to divine counsel and instruction will ultimately ensure that we enjoy the benefits of the covenant relationship in famine and through lifetime. This obedience is God's secret code to abundance.

You may know you need to sow. But divine instruction is what tells you where (the best place) to plant that seed.

When you OBEY God, you will not only enjoy His abundance but also His peace. God Bless.

"Who is wise and understanding among you? Let him show by good conduct that his works are done in the meekness of wisdom. [14] But if you have bitter envy and self-seeking in your hearts, do not boast and lie against the truth. [15] This wisdom does not descend from above, but is earthly, sensual, demonic. [16] For where envy and self-seeking exist, confusion and every evil thing are there. [17] But the wisdom that is from above is first pure, then peaceable, gentle, willing to yield, full of mercy and good fruits, without partiality and without hypocrisy. [18] Now the fruit of righteousness is sown in peace by those who make peace. **James 3: 13-18**

SO HOW DO WE USE THE POWER OF OBEDIENCE TO LIVE IN KINGDOM WEALTH?

The Bible says in 2 Timothy 3:7 that there are folks who are: "Ever learning, and never able to come to the knowledge of the truth".

This means you can learn all you want and still not know the truth. So, you can be well educated in error.

This is not a word against education. It simply means God cannot be found in Education, but in His word. Don't confuse the two or mix them up. Because you are educated does not mean you know the Truth from the Word. With all your getting...get into the word.

Many believers have knowledge but still don't know the Truth.

"Sanctify them in the truth; your word is truth." John 17:17

"Jesus answered, "I am the way and the truth and the life. No one comes to the Father except through me." John 14:6

There is no Truth without Christ; regardless of the knowledge you have accumulated. We need to understand the concept of the Kingdom if we are to access true Abundance on the earth.

All Kingdom economies are called COMMONWEALTH and not Capitalism. Kingdoms have commonwealth and not capitalism. WHY?

When God created Adam, He gave him RULERSHIP over the earth and not OWNERSHIP. Managers are not Owners. Stewards are not Owner

Adam was given stewardship over the earth and not ownership. Dominion in the kingdom does not mean ownership.

We are not supposed to OWN anything on the earth. This is where many believers have problems. We are supposed to manage it, develop it, refine it, cultivate it, multiply it and dominate it; but never own it.

So, the Spirit of OWNERSHIP is what causes our FEAR & Troubles materially on the earth. POVERTY is a result of OWNERSHIP.

If we can tune the heaven's frequency, we can see that Adam was not given ownership, He WAS GIVEN ACCESS.

"A river flowed out of Eden to water the garden, and there it divided and became four rivers. The name of the first is the Pishon. It is the one that flowed around the whole land of Havilah, where there is gold. And the gold of that land is good; bdellium and onyx stone are there. 13 The name of the second river is the Gihon. It is the one that flowed around the whole land of Cush. And the name of the third river is the Tigris, which flows east of Assyria. And the fourth river is the Euphrates.
The LORD God took the man and put him in the garden of Eden to work it and keep it. 16 And the LORD God commanded the man, saying, "You may surely eat of every tree of the garden, but of the tree of the knowledge of good and evil you

shall not eat, for in the day that you eat[d] of it you shall surely die." **Genesis 2:10-17** (ESV):

Adam was INSTRUCTED to WORK it and KEEP (LOOK AFTER) it. God never said he should own it.

Abundance in the Kingdom of God is about ACCESS to God's limitless resources and never about OWNERSHIP by man.

Access means freedom to possess and enjoy without worry about production and supply. Production and supply of what is to be consumed is where the real trouble is. Access is easy.

This does not mean you will do nothing and be idle. It simply means your work or actions merely accesses what is already supplied.

Many of us have grown up in a DEMOCRACY and brought up in CAPITALISM; so tuning to the Kingdom paradigm of access is problematic for many.

If I give you the access keys to a big shopping Mall. And I say you can go in and get anything you want at any time for the rest of your life. How will you feel?

- ✓ Freedom from worry
- ✓ Relaxed
- ✓ Prosperous
- ✓ Restful
- ✓ Peaceful….etc…

It seems like believers like stress and struggle too much. We want to own things (with all the trouble that it attracts) instead of using our access to what is already provided.

QUESTION: If you have £1000 cash on you for shopping and I have no money but have access to the Shopping Mall (to take anything I need); Who is more prosperous? You or Me?

God does not want you to own anything; He want to grant you access to what He owns. So,

He uses the tiny little you own to test your readiness to access the abundance that He owns. Commonwealth means all the citizens have access for what they need, but nobody owns anything.

- ✓ The key to all Kingdoms is the KING.
- ✓ The King own everything in a Kingdom.

Owner is from the Hebrew word ADON. ADON literally mean LORD. That is why the person you rent from is still called "LandLORD".

We are not the LORD of the resources we need, God is. He is the Lord of ALL things. The word LORD in the Bible is not a title. It is a Designation of Ownership.

The Earth is the Lords' MEANS God is the owner of the earth and all things in it. The Kingdom's greatest strength is the fact that there is no private ownership. We simply use Obedience to His instructions to access what belongs to the King.

"And the LORD God commanded the man, saying, "You may freely (unconditionally) eat [the fruit] from every tree of the garden." **Genesis 2:16** (AMP)

Adam was granted FREE access not ownership. "…You can FREELY Eat" God said.

Worry is only possible where ownership is present. Sin separated us from the Commonwealth God owns. But Jesus came to fix that.

"Remember that at that time you were separated from Christ [excluded from any relationship with Him], alienated from the commonwealth of Israel, and strangers to the covenants of promise [with no share in the sacred Messianic promise and without knowledge of God's agreements], having no hope [in His promise] and [living] in the world without God. 13 BUT NOW [at this very moment] in Christ Jesus you who once were [so very] far away [from God] have been brought near [a]by the blood of Christ. 14 For

*He Himself is our peace and our bond of unity.
He who made both groups—[Jews and
Gentiles]—into one body and broke down the
barrier, the dividing wall [of spiritual
antagonism between us]"* **Ephesians 2:12-14**
(AMP)

COMMONWEALTH DEFINED

Commonwealth is the Constitutional obligation
of a King to the welfare of His citizens. It is the
Common access by citizens to the Bountiful
resources of the Wealth of the economy of the
King of the Kingdom.

The Prodigal Son, asked his father to "give me
what is MINE." The Son though had access
wanted ownership. That was the beginning of his
stress and trouble.

Trouble is: If you own something, when it is
gone you own NOTHING.

So, when all was lost, the Bible says he came to himself.

The FIRST Step to Kingdom ACCESS (out of lack and poverty and to access the commonwealth of God) is SELF VISITATION.

What am I doing here struggling when my father owns everything? The Prodigal Son then said, "I will Arise and go…"

The SECOND step is that you have got to INITIATE you own Action.

Do you notice that in this story, the father never went looking for the son?

You have got to start the process yourself. You have got to start living a life of Obedience. You have got to let go of what you own and access what you can steward (limitless).

I will ARISE…. Initiate the change yourself.

Have you had enough of the stress of this world system? **Then start the action now.**

...ARISE.....and go.

You have access to God's unlimited resources. Stop limiting yourself through ownership.

"Therefore I say unto you, Take no thought for your life, what ye shall eat, or what ye shall drink; nor yet for your body, what ye shall put on. Is not the life more than meat, and the body than raiment? Behold the fowls of the air: for they sow not, neither do they reap, nor gather into barns; yet your heavenly Father feedeth them. Are ye not much better than they?

Which of you by taking thought can add one cubit unto his stature? And why take ye thought for raiment? Consider the lilies of the field, how they grow; they toil not, neither do they spin: And yet I say unto you, That even Solomon in all his glory was not arrayed like one of these.

Wherefore, if God so clothe the grass of the field, which to day is, and to morrow is cast into the oven, shall he not much more clothe you, O ye of little faith?

Therefore take no thought, saying, What shall we eat? or, What shall we drink? or, Wherewithal shall we be clothed?

(For after all these things do the Gentiles seek:) for your heavenly Father knoweth that ye have need of all these things. (THEREFORE HE OWNS & SUPPLY THEM ALREADY). But seek ye first the kingdom of God, and his righteousness; and all these things shall be added unto you.

Take therefore no thought for the morrow: for the morrow shall take thought for the things of itself. Sufficient unto the day is the evil thereof."
Matthew 6:25-34 (KJV)

Obedience therefore is the key to living in abundance using God's secret code. What His secret code will do is lead you to where His hidden riches are for you to steward. The better your stewardship the more God will give you to look after.

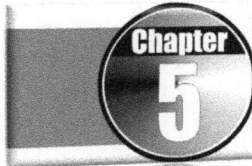

THE
RIGHTEOUSNESS FACTOR

To end this book, I will like to address a major reason many Believers do not tap into this 'secret code' for abundance. Like I stated before, we produce fruit of Righteousness which is Obedience; this leads us to the hidden riches as we walk in divine guidance.

But a lot of Believers feel such accomplishment is reserved for the "Big Men and Women" of God. That it is reserved for "Ministers". This is not correct. We ALL have access to code as we received this same righteousness as children of God. We may be more mature than each other; we are not more righteous that each other.

The righteousness which is by grace is made available to all mankind equally. The Cross of Christ is a leveller. We are all the same at the foot of the cross. I therefore feel I need to address the righteousness factor as it is essential to our confidence in developing fruit that will last and endure.

The Bible says that if we confess our sins, God is faithful and just to forgive us our sins and cleanse us from all unrighteousness. The bible does not say God will give us a new righteousness.

Sin can make you break fellowship with God but it does not stop you being righteous because righteousness of God in Christ Jesus is irreversible. Sin can make you break fellowship just like your son if he does something very bad you may decide not to talk to him for the next two hours, but that does not stop him from being your son. He will still answer to your name.

You may say you don't want to see him today, because you are angry about that particular situation. But if someone were to call him by your name, he will answer because that does not change regardless of the specific wrongdoing.

And that is what it means to be the righteousness of God in Christ Jesus; but the difficulties that many children of God have is that they don't understand how strong this principle is.

If someone says to you that you may be the son of the king of Saudi, until you are clearly able to ascertain this, there are certain things you can't do. It might raise your hopes but you can't start forcing certain doors to open if you don't have proof that you are a Prince.

Before we can fully walk in OBEDIENCE to God; we have to resolve the issue of righteousness otherwise whenever you step out of line and the devil makes you feel that you are no longer the righteousness of God, you will cede your authority.

Anyone who feels that way can't exercise authority, so it is important we settle this, so that you understand that it is God's will for you to have certain things.

"Hear O Israel; thou art to pass over Jordan this day, to go in to possess nations greater and mightier than thyself, cities great and fenced up to heaven" **Deuteronomy 9:1.**

The instruction here is that they are to go and possess nations greater and mightier than themselves. That is the mission of mankind on earth – they are greater and mightier than yourself but they are not greater and mightier than your God.

It's important you understand what God is about to do and get your confidence back in your pursuit of Godly obedience. Walking hand in hand with Jehovah, you are unstoppable.

You need to build your confidence in God and not in yourself. Your God is the Lion of the tribe of Judah, the One who is the ever-present help in time of need. Heaven is His throne and the earth His footstool; He is the unchanging changer; the all-seeing and all-knowing God. If God is for you "who" can be against you? Be bold my friend and go and take the land.

"A people great and tall, the descendants of the Anakim, whom you know, and of whom you heard it said, 'Who can stand before the descendants of Anak?'". **Deuteronomy 9:2.**

Sometimes I use this verse, when telling people who are starting their own business not to be afraid; it's your job, your commission to go and dispossess nations bigger than yourself, the multinationals, of this world, they are yours for the taking. The bible calls them tall and giants.

God will lead you to pleasant places. That leading becomes His secret code.

"Therefore, understand today that the LORD your God is He who goes over before you as a consuming fire. He will destroy them and bring them down before you; so you shall drive them out and destroy them quickly, as the LORD has said to you.[4] *"Do not think in your heart, after the LORD your God has cast them out before you, saying, 'Because of my righteousness the LORD has brought me in to possess this land'; but it is because of the wickedness of these nations that the LORD is driving them out from before you.* [5] *It is not because of your righteousness or the uprightness of your heart that you go in to possess their land, but because of the wickedness of these nations that the LORD your God drives them out from before you, and that He may fulfil the word which the LORD swore to your fathers, to Abraham, Isaac, and Jacob.* [6] *Therefore understand that the LORD your God is not giving you this good land to*

possess because of your righteousness, for you are a stiff-necked people. **Deuteronomy 9:3-6**

God is still giving you these victories, even though you are described as stiff necked. The question is why is He doing it if he considers you as stiff necked. He made it clear it's not because of your righteousness. For us to understand righteousness you need to see certain events in the bible so that you understand the awesomeness of the God we serve.

Jacob and Laban:
"So shall my righteousness answer for me in time to come, when it shall come for my hire before thy face; everyone that is not speckled and spotted among the goats, and brown among the sheep, that shall be counted stolen with me". **Genesis 30 verse 33**

He said his righteousness would speak for him in the time to come. So, note the word 'Righteousness' here.

Again, we see the same in the story of **Abimelech**.

"But Abimelech had not yet come near her: and he said "Lord, wilt thou slay also a righteous nation?" **Genesis 20:4**

He said – I did this in the integrity of my heart.

The reason for these two examples is because the righteousness referred to in these two verses is what I call *"conformity with moral law"* it is not the righteousness that produces fruit of Obedience; it is not the righteousness of God in Christ Jesus.

When Jacob said my "righteousness" he meant his honesty. This is observance of human law. The question is which righteousness do you live and win by? The righteousness you win by is not what you call honesty or by just doing the right thing.

Exodus Chapter 15: 1, 12-13 – the song of Moses states:

*"Then sang Moses and the children of Israel this song unto the Lord and spake saying: "I will sing unto the Lord for He has triumphed gloriously, the horse and rider hath he thrown into the sea. The Lord is my strength and song, and He is become my salvation he is my God and I will prepare him an inhabitation; my father's God, and I will exalt him. The Lord is a man of war, the Lord is His name". "thou stretchedst out thy right hand, the earth swallowed them". "Thou in thy mercy hast led forth the people which thou has redeemed; thou has guided them in **thy strength** unto thy holy habitation"*

Key point here is you have guided them in <u>Your strength</u>. Not in their own strength, but in 'Your strength'.

Also, 1Sam 2:1,9 the song of Hannah declared:.
"And Hannah prayed and said, my heart rejoiceth in the Lord, mine heart is exalted in the Lord; my mouth is enlarged over mine

*enemies because I rejoice in thy salvation". "He will guard the feet of His saints, but the wicked shall be silent in darkness; for **by strength shall no man prevail**".*

So, Moses said God guided them in his strength alone and Hannah also said "for by strength shall no man prevail".

WHAT IS THE RIGHTEOUSNESS THAT PRODUCES FRUIT OF OBEDIENCE?

*"Brethren my hearts desire and prayer to God for Israel is that they might be saved. For I bear them record that they have a zeal of God, but not according to knowledge, for they being ignorant, of **God's righteousness,** and seeking to establish **their own righteousness** have not submitted themselves unto the **righteousness of God"**.* ROMANS 10:1

In this verse, you can see the Bible has mentioned two types of righteousness. They are following their own righteousness which is observance or following human laws, regulations, or edicts. It is important to understand that operating in the righteousness of God is not observance of human laws.

If you do not understand fully that you are operating in the righteousness of God or you do not understand the ramifications of that statement, you will not be able to OBEY God's instructions; because you will always be cowed by the deceptions and accusations of the enemy.

Isaiah 51 verse 1: *"Hearken to me ye that **follow after righteousness**, ye that seek the Lord; look unto the rock whence ye are hewn, and to the hole of the pit whence ye are digged. Look to Abraham your fathers and unto Sarah that bare you; for I called him alone, and blessed him, and increased him".*

Verse 5: *"My righteousness is near; my salvation is gone forth, and mine arms shall judge the people; the isles shall wait upon me, and on mine arm shall they trust".*

Verse 7: *"Hearken unto me, ye that **know righteousness**, the people whose heart is my law; hear ye not the reproach of men, neither be ye afraid of their reviling"*.

Are you following after righteousness or do you know righteousness? Do you know Him.

THERE ARE 3 TYPES OF RIGHTEOUSNESS:

Righteousness of man which produces filthiness.

"But we are all as an unclean thing, and all our righteousnesses are like filthy rags; Isaiah 64:6.

This is when people want to use their will to do the right thing. There are some people who are not saved but are good people. They observe all the laws of man – this is the righteousness of man which the bible says is as "filthy rags".

The righteousness of man on the face of it might seem okay, but God considers it as filthiness. It is important that you understand that it is not the righteousness by which we operate or win by.

The second type of **righteousness is the righteousness of the law**. Righteousness which produces consciousness of sin.

Romans 3 verse 20. *"Therefore by the deeds of the law there shall no flesh be justified in His sight; for by the law is the knowledge of sin"*.

The third type of righteousness is the **RIGHTEOUSNESS OF FAITH**. This is the righteousness of God, the righteousness to live by. The one that produces fruit of obedience.

*"But now **the righteousness of God without the law is manifested**, being witnessed by the law and the prophets; even the righteousness of God which is by faith of Jesus Christ unto all and upon all them that believe; for there is no difference; for all have sinned and come short of*

*the glory of God. Being justified freely by His grace through the redemption that is in Christ Jesus; whom God hath set forth to be a **propitiation through faith** in His blood, to declare His righteousness for the remission of sins that are past, through the forbearance of God".* **Romans 3:21–25**

Every believer has the same righteousness. Assume we have a group of three people who are all male for the purpose of this illustration. Two of them are well known Pastors and the other a new Christian; all three people have the same level of righteousness.

We need to understand that when they are standing to proclaim access to what God has, they all have equal access.

As Christians, we have developed a dependency culture whereby we feel we need to talk to a Pastor, who will then talk to God on our behalf. We all have access to God equally.

Clearly people are more mature than others and that maturity brings knowledge that allows you to be able to enjoy the reality of redemption more than another; but that does not change the fundamental fact that we are all in Christ equally righteousness.

From this illustration, it is clear that although one person's walk with God might be deeper than another, it does not change the fact that we all have equal access to God from the platform of faith in God.

It is important that you don't think that one person is more righteous than the other; you are as righteous as the man preaching on TV, you are as righteous as that man who wrote that best-selling gospel book; every believer has the same righteousness.

We can practice righteousness more than each other due to maturity in God and knowledge of Him, but we all have the same righteousness of faith in Christ Jesus. This is what is needed to bear fruit of obedience. You are not inferior to anybody.

What you see when people manifest Gods presence more than others is not increase in righteousness, but increase in maturity. It is very important that you understand you are as righteous as that man or woman of God you admire.

OPERATING IN OBEDIENCE THROUGH THE RIGHTEOUSNESS OF GOD

"Now we know that whatever the law says, it says to those who are under the law, that every mouth may be stopped, and all the world may become guilty before God. Therefore by the deeds of the law no flesh will be justified in His sight, for by the law is the knowledge of sin. But now the righteousness of God apart from the law is revealed, being witnessed by the Law and the Prophets, even the righteousness of God, through faith in Jesus Christ, to all and on all

who believe. For there is no difference."
Romans 3:19 – 22

Understand this clearly in your mind: **"what did not obtain righteousness for you cannot then take it away from you".** The righteousness of God is not a temporary activity it is permanent.

Did you become the righteousness of God by stopping smoking, not lying, by being honest? Those are not the things that got you righteous, **you got the righteousness by faith in Christ Jesus.**

What did not get you the righteousness cannot take it away from you. When you sin, you break fellowship, because you run away from God (He never runs away from us), but you are still the righteousness of God in Christ Jesus, because not sinning did not get you there in the first place.

Do not listen to the lie of the devil, whereby he is able to hang a sin over your head like a sword and every time you want to exercise your authority or OBEY God, he brings it to your remembrance. You can tell him to shut up because your not sinning did not obtain you righteousness in the first place.

If as you thought before, when you sin God just cut you off complete; how would He be able to hear you when you confess your sins? He that covers his sins will not prosper, but if we confess our sins He is faithful and just to forgive us all our sins and forgive us all unrighteousness.

The question is while we are confessing our sins how is He able to hear if we are not within earshot of Him. If suddenly every time you sin, God exports you somewhere far away on a one-way ticket; how will He know you are sorry?

When you say you are sorry and God hears you and forgives you, it's on the basis of you being His righteousness has not changed even though you sinned.

Yes, fellowship might have been affected by your running away, but your being His righteousness is by faith in Christ Jesus and not according to the law. Amen.

You need to understand this very carefully and develop boldness for dominion in life. This boldness is what is needed for you to Obey God as Isaac, Jacob and David did.

To wrap this up, there are FIVE THINGS YOU MUST UNDERSTAND about operating in the righteousness of God.

1.   Every time you look at the subject of righteousness one thing should always be on your mind: **"What is at stake is your justification"?** This means it is either we are justified by faith or not at all. We are righteous for no other reason than that God has declared us righteous. God has declared you justified.

Romans Chapter 3 verse 20 states:

"Therefore by the deeds of the law there shall no flesh be justified in his sight: for by the law is the knowledge of sin". In other words you are righteous for no other reason than the fact that God has declared you righteous."

And the gifts and calling of God are without repentance. You need to hold on to this. The bible says that *"For the lord has commended his love towards us in that while we were still sinners, He died for us"*. Christ already died for the ungodly.

The people going around today saying there is no God; Christ has already died for them. God's relationship with man is not "I love you because you love me". God's relationship with man is *"I love you, full stop"*.

Even though man does not yet love God, even though man may be denying the existence of God; God is saying I still love you anyway. If that is the case for people who don't agree God exists, how much more you who have now been sanctified by the blood of the Lamb.

God does not love you because you are a nice man or woman, or because of what you have done, He just loves you. Nothing else matters. It is absolutely important that you understand what justification means. God has declared you justified and it is on this basis that you have become the righteousness of God in Christ Jesus.

It is irreversible. It is important therefore that you come to a knowledge that it does not matter what sin you have committed, you can still go boldly to the throne of grace, confess your sins and begin to declare what God wants you to declare. You cannot live in obedience on earth if you are cowed by the fear of sins you have committed in the past. That is the tactic of the enemy.

2. **You cannot earn God's righteousness;** it is His act of grace through Christ Jesus. 2 Cor 5 verse 16 *"From now on, regard no one*

according to the flesh, yea though we have known Christ after the flesh, yet now henceforth know we Him no more. Therefore if anyone is in Christ, he is a new creation, old things have passed away; behold all things are become new. Now all things are of God who hath reconciled us to Himself by Jesus Christ, and hat given to us the ministry of reconciliation. To wit, that God was in Christ, reconciling the world unto himself not imputing their trespasses unto them; and hath committed unto us the word of reconciliation".

You cannot earn God's righteousness it is an act of Grace through Jesus Christ. John 3:16 says *"For God so loved the world that He gave His only begotten son that whosever believes in Him should not perish but have everlasting life".*

This is a one-way traffic in that God commended His love towards us, it cannot be earned. When you realise this; you know that you have to begin to deal with things that cut fellowship, but never shirk from the fact that you are the righteousness of God in Christ Jesus.

Grace is not simply leniency when we have sinned. Grace is the enabling gift of God not to sin. Grace is power, not just pardon. Therefore, the effort we make to obey God is not an effort done in our own strength, but in the strength which God supplies. This obedience is what gives us access to His secret code.

The duties God requires of us are not in proportion to the strength we possess in ourselves. Rather, they are proportional to the resources available to us in Christ. We do not have the ability in ourselves to accomplish the least of God's tasks. This is a law of grace. When we recognise it is impossible to perform a duty in our own strength, we will discover the secret of its accomplishment

You must not question the fundamentals of whether you are the righteousness of God in Christ Jesus. God who does not waiver gave it to you. Once you accept Christ you are the righteousness of God in Christ Jesus.

3. **If I am the righteousness of God, what happens when I sin?** If and when you sin, **it does nothing to your righteousness**. When we sin we break fellowship because we tend to run from God. Your 'sinlessness' did not make you righteousness if you are a born again child of God; so you need to regain your boldness in God. This confidence is needed to obey God.

"This is the message which we have heard of Him and declare unto you, that God is light, and in Him is no darkness at all. If we say that we have fellowship with Him, and walk in darkness, we lie, and do not the truth: but if we walk in the light, as He is in the light, we have fellowship with one another and the blood of Jesus Christ His Son cleanseth us from all sin. If we say we have no sin, we deceive ourselves, and the truth is not in us. If we confess our sins, He is faithful and just to forgive us our sins, and to cleanse us from all unrighteousness". **1 John 1: 5-8**

Verse 8 tells us we will be cleansed from all unrighteousness not that we will be made righteous again.

In Zachariah 3:1-2, talking about the vision of Christ to come, the bible says *"And he shewed me Joshua the high priest standing before the angel of the Lord and satan standing at the right hand to resist him. And the Lord said unto satan, The Lord rebuke thee o Satan; even the Lord that hath chosen Jerusalem rebuke thee is this not a brand plucked from the fire, now Joshua was clothed with filthy garments and was standing before the angel. And He answered and spake unto those that stood before Him, saying, take away the filthy garments from him"*.

"I will greatly rejoice in the Lord, my soul shall be joyful in my God: for He hath clothed me with the garments of salvation, he hath covered me with the robe of righteousness, as a bridegroom decketh himself with ornaments, and as a bride adorneth herself with jewels". **Isaiah 61 :10**

God exchanged our filthy garments for robes of righteousness. When you sin, you do not need a new robe, you only need to clean the one you have.

When you sin it's as if there is a spot on your robe, and you get detergent and clean that dirt away and your robe is okay again. That is what the Blood of Jesus has done for us. It is very important for you to understand this.

4.   **Believers do not put on a robe any more, we put on a person and His name is Jesus, He is our Righteousness, He is our Redemption and He is our Justification.**

1 Corinthians 1:30 states; *"But of Him are ye in Christ Jesus, who of God is made unto us wisdom, and righteousness, and sanctification and redemption"*

Isaiah 51 verse 1: *"Hearken to me ye that follow after righteousness, ye that seek the Lord; look unto the rock whence ye are hewn,* *and to the hole of the pit whence ye are digged. Look to Abraham your fathers and unto Sarah that bare you; for I called him alone, and blessed him, and increased him".*

Verse 7: *"Hearken unto me, ye that **know righteousness**, the people whose heart is my law; hear ye not the reproach of men, neither be ye afraid of their reviling".*

Isaiah 51 verse 1 talks of those who follow after righteous while verse 7 talks about those who know righteousness.

We now understand that righteousness is a person, i.e. Christ. **All some people do is follow after Christ, they don't really know Him.** And those are the people who try to observe rules and regulations, but once you know righteousness, you know Christ personally and following and obeying Him becomes a lot easier.

It is important for you to understand that New Testament saints don't put on robes anymore, we put on a person and His name is Jesus. Hence, as He is in heaven so are we on earth.

2 Corinthians 5 verse 21 states; *"For He made Him who knew no sin, to become sin for us, that we might become the righteousness of God in Christ Jesus"*

5.   **Why was Jesus made sin?** Because **if Jesus was going to have legal right to access hell He needed to become sin.** Jesus would not have been able to go to hell if he was sinless. That would not follow the law, so our sins were imputed on Him. The wages of sin is death, so He paid the price, the word of God has to be obeyed.

The bible says God put all of that on Jesus and killed Him. That way the word of God is fulfilled that says *"the soul that sins must die."* But by being resurrected and we now believing in Him, we are now no longer supposed to be paying the price because the price has already been paid.

That is why when you sin today you can ask for forgiveness knowing that you will not die, because someone else has already paid the price.

On the way, out of hell Christ shut the door against those that are righteous. He alone maintains our righteousness. **You stand in all that God is and all that God has you must not be intimidated any more.** Rise up boldly and understand that you are as righteous as any man of God on the face of this earth.

Because Christ does not discriminate, they may be more mature than you but you can develop yourself as well. However, the fundamentals are the same.

Righteousness is the ability to stand before God without a sense of shame, guilt or inferiority. This is essential to sharpen your ability to hear God and most importantly your willingness to OBEY His instructions.

We need to know righteousness which is Jesus Christ, we then need to believe in our hearts what He has said and we need to declare with our mouth what the word says about us. That is the only way.

What is rightfully yours is yours by virtue of your righteousness in Christ Jesus. Satan is called the accuser of the brethren because that is all he has. You need to have an answer for Satan and that is that you are the righteousness of God in Christ Jesus. The devil specialises in trying to sell you what you already have.

Deception is the number one tool of the enemy. You must therefore understand that he still uses the same trick today.

As I end this book; I hope you can see that you; yes, you reading these words can boldly and in confidence OBEY the commands of God regardless of your situation. This Obedience becomes the fruit with which you access the hidden riches.

These riches in heavenly places in Christ Jesus are kept there so the enemy cannot reach them. But they are translated into the physical realm as and when you need it. The location it is transferred into is what God will instruct you on. The process of instructing you as to where to go to requires your Obedience. This is God's secret code to abundance.

Simply sowing and reaping on the earth will still be needed as we are here on earth. We have to obey the rules of this realm. But in addition to this; God will lead you to places where you will take possession of fields you did not plant, vineyards you did not cultivate.

"So I gave you a land on which you did not toil and cities you did not build; and you live in them and eat from vineyards and olive groves that you did not plant." **Joshua 24:13**

"The houses will be richly stocked with goods you did not produce. You will draw water from cisterns you did not dig, and you will eat from

vineyards and olive trees you did not plant. When you have eaten your fill in this land" **Deut 6:11**

"I sent you to reap what you have not worked for. Others have done the hard work, and you have reaped the benefits of their labor." **John 4:38**

These scriptures evidences how heaven's supply comes into your life. It is not be your labour. God instructs you. And your obedience, just like that of Isaac; will be the fruit of righteousness that you will sow to prosper beyond those who do not know God. This is your distinguishing factor.

This is you enjoying a release from heaven that has been translated into the physical. Through favour and mercy, God will prosper you.

So, walk confidently in the righteousness which is rooted in Christ Jesus. God bless you.

BONUS MATERIAL

HOW WRONG THOUGHTS AND EMOTIONS BREED DISOBEDIENCE

✓ *Understanding that your thoughts create your realities*

✓ *Divine strategies for developing a healthy and renewed mind.*

✓ *Learning to Obey God and unlocking your potential through the power of a renewed mind.*

THE PLACE OF THE HUMAN SPIRIT IN AIDING OUR ABILITY TO OBEY GOD

Understanding Obedience through the Development of the Human Spirit

Wrong Mindset leads to wrong thoughts, wrong thoughts leads to wrong emotions and wrong emotions lead to wrong living. In this book, I want to show you things about yourself that you might never have fully grasped until now. Things about how God relates and communicates with us.

We know quite clearly from 1 Thessalonians 5:23 that man is a spirit, he has a soul and he lives in a body. Please take all references to man in this book to mean mankind (both male and female).

1 Thessalonians 5:23 – *"Now may the God of peace Himself sanctify you entirely; and may your spirit and soul and body be preserved complete, without blame at the coming of our Lord Jesus Christ."*

In Genesis 1:26, the Bible says that God created man in His image and after His likeness. And in Genesis 2:7 we read that God formed man out of the dust of the earth.

The man that God formed in Genesis 2 is just the physical body, the man that God created in Genesis 1 is the real man; he is the spiritual entity that has a complete likeness to God.

So, when God formed man in Genesis 2, he put the spirit which he had earlier created inside that body and when the two came together, the soul was formed. The soul of man is a combination of the influences of the spirit and the body.

Whether you are a believer or not, you still have 3 parts to you. You have the Spirit, the Body and then between the two you have the Soul.

This is the tripartite combination of everybody whether you are a believer or not. The difference for unbelievers is that their spirit is dead to God but is alive to the spirit world of the devil.

This should not be taken as a gruesome picture of all unbelievers congregating and worshipping the devil. But clearly, the bible says, to whom you yield your body, you are a slave to.

As believers, we are slaves to righteousness, while unbelievers are slaves to iniquity or lawlessness. The Bible talk about strong meat is for those who by reason of use have had their senses exercised.

Hebrews 5:12-14 (KJV) - *For when for the time ye ought to be teachers, ye have need that one teach you again which be the first principles of the oracles of God; and are become such as have need of milk, and not of strong meat. For every* *one that useth milk is unskilful in the word of righteousness: for he is a babe. But strong meat belongeth to them that are of full age, even those who by reason of use have their senses exercised to discern both good and evil.*

You can be an unbeliever and yet exercise your spirit in such a way that you are very alive to the demonic spirit world.

That is why you have witches, sorcerers and people of that ilk who can look at you and tell you hidden and strange things because even though they are unbelievers they have trained their human spirit to communicate better with the evil spirit world.

Just like you have dormant unbelievers, you have active unbelievers. That is, you have unbelievers whose spirits are not sensitive even though they have access to the evil world, they are not actively pursuing it. And you have those who are actively pursuing it and are thus more sensitive.

In the same way, you have inactive believers who although their spirits are alive to God, are not utilising it. Likewise, you have those who are active believers and fervently pursuing God and thus training their spirits and are able to get more information from God.

The point I am making is that spirit, soul and body is the same whether you are a believer or not. The difference is that your spirit is alive to God when you are a believer.

When you are an unbeliever, your soul is so much wrapped up with the body and its fruits that your spirit is practically neglected and that is why you tend to follow your own will and its lustful desires.

With your body, you relate to the physical world, with your spirit you relate to the spiritual world and with your soul, you relate with the intellectual world in what is called, self-consciousness.

In Genesis chapter 2 verse 7, the Bible says
...man became a living soul. In the Bible,
sometimes the word soul is substituted for the
word life, to mean the number of people. This
means that you are what your soul is. Even
though you are a believer, it is the information
contained in your soul that defines who you are
experientially.

That is why I said, wrong mind leads to wrong
thought; wrong thought leads to wrong emotion
and wrong emotion leads to wrong living.

Your spirit cannot communicate directly with
your body neither can your body communicate
directly with your spirit. The carnal values
which the body represents cannot relate with the
consecration contained in a renewed human
spirit. The two cannot relate.

Therefore, they both communicate and
consolidate their desires via the soul. Hence the
battleground for the future of mankind is in our
soul. The Bible says if any man be in Christ, he

is a new creature, old things are passed away and all things have become new. What is remaining of the old person in you or the old lifestyle in you is your memory.

In which case, you can still become a slave to your old memory, even though you are now saved. Whoever wins the soul battle wins the control over your life. Your soul makes it possible for your spiritual values to impact your body and be maintained by it. It is important that you understand that fact.

FUNCTIONS OF THE HUMAN SPIRIT
The human spirit has three main functions. Human beings have spirits, this is separate from the Holy Spirit; you have a spirit as a human being. The three functions are:
❖   Conscience function,
❖   Intuition function and
❖   Communion function.

COMPONENTS OF THE HUMAN SPIRIT

These are the three main functions of your spirit. Proverbs 25:28, Hebrews. 12:23, Zech. 12:1, Rom. 8:16, these are just some of the scriptures that prove that man has a spirit.

1 Corinthians 2:11 – *"For who among men knows the thoughts of a man except the spirit of the man which is in him? Even so the thoughts of God no one knows except the Spirit of God."*

Clearly the scripture here distinguishes between the spirit of man within and the Spirit of God. They are two separate entities. Human beings do have spirits.

THE CONSCIENCE FUNCTION.

Your conscience is the discerning organ which distinguishes right from wrong. This is what makes it different. It does not distinguish right from wrong from what I call stored knowledge but it is a spontaneous direct judgment based on the spirit of God.

Your conscience does not discern right from wrong based solely on your mental knowledge. Sometimes you are faced with something that you don't have the full knowledge of, but you know it is still wrong. That is your conscience speaking. It is a spontaneous action.

You are about to do something and even though it is legal on paper based on natural laws but your conscience still tells you it is wrong. Abortion is legal in most countries, isn't it?

But if you attempt to go and abort, you will hear your conscience telling you not to do it. Since, the natural human law says it is okay, then you are most likely not getting the check as a result of stored knowledge of wrong, it is something inside you telling you that it is wrong.

There are so many decisions we make on a day to day basis. The work of conscience is independent and it is direct. It does not bend to outside opinions. It is not influenced by your soul, or your body. What evidence is there of conscience? If you do wrong it will raise its voice of conviction, which is what the conscience does.

John 13:21 – *"when Jesus had said this, he became troubled in spirit." That is His conscience that is working. It is his conscience making that communication with Him."*

Acts 17:16 – *"Now, while Paul was waiting for them at Athens, his spirit was being stirred up within him." Again that is the conscience that is working. Your conscience is the discerner that distinguishes right from wrong."*

2Cor. 2:13 – *"I had no rest for my spirit, not finding Titus my brother; but taking my leave of them, I went on to Macedonia."*

The second function of your human spirit is what is called the intuition function.

THE INTUITION FUNCTION.

Intuition is the sensing organ of the human spirit. Intuition involves a direct sensing devoid of any outside influences. That which comes to us without any help from the mind, emotion or volition comes intuitively. Your intuition is what communicates with the Spirit of God. Every information you obtain in your spirit you get via your intuition. It is just that many times we need a mature mind to be in the right position to interpret that information.

Have you ever been in a situation where you just woke up in the morning and you are troubled in your spirit maybe to pray for somebody? You don't know what is happening, you don't know the problem the person has, but you just have that feeling to pray for this person.

What is happening in your spirit is that your intuition is picking up heaven's frequency, the Spirit of God is talking to your spirit but because your mind cannot interpret that information yet, you don't know the details.

Maybe the next day you find out that the person was going through some difficulty at that time or you find out that some armed robbers were about to invade that person's house. You didn't know all that information at the time you were praying; but your intuition got the input directly from the Spirit of God.

The Holy Spirit does not speak to the human mind. The Holy Spirit cannot, does not and will not communicate with human soul. He can only communicate with our spirit. It is our spirit that relays that information to our mind and our mind then interprets it.

The revelation of God and the movement of the Holy Spirit are known to the believers only through their intuition. A believer needs to heed the voice of conscience and the teaching of intuition.

Others may call it discernment, but it does not really matter. The important thing is to be aware of the function and not be bogged down with designation.

Evidence of intuition function is in the Bible.

Mark 2:8 - Immediately Jesus, aware in His spirit that they were reasoning that way within themselves, said to them, "Why are you reasoning about these things in your hearts?

John 11:33 – *"When Jesus therefore saw her weeping, and the Jews who came with her also weeping, He was deeply moved in spirit and was troubled."*

Acts 18:5 (KJV) – *"And when Silas and Timotheus were come from Macedonia, Paul was pressed in the spirit, and testified to the Jews that Jesus was Christ."*

Acts 20:22 (AMP) – *"And now, you see, I am going to Jerusalem, bound by the [Holy] Spirit and obligated and compelled by the [convictions of my own] spirit, not knowing what will befall me there."*

In Acts 20:22, Paul knew something was wrong. The Holy Spirit has already spoken to him quite clearly that this journey is going to be a difficult one.

His intuition had received the information and his mind had not fully interpreted it so he did not know exactly what was waiting for him where he was going; other than the fact that there will be trouble.

The third component of the human spirit is communion.

COMMUNION.
Communion is the third function of the human spirit. Our soul is incompetent to worship God. God cannot be apprehended by our thoughts, feelings or intentions; but He can only be known directly in our spirits.

What the bible calls "the inner man". True worship is first of all a spiritual connection with God. Our soul can magnify the Lord; but it cannot worship God.

Because our souls are incompetent to worship God, true worship takes place in our spirit. God does not communicate with the human soul, as I have explained earlier. Our spirit picks up signals and messages and our souls bring mental understanding of that signal.

The deep calls to the deep. The Spirit always communicates only with the spirit. God's Spirit cannot communicate with our soul. If the Holy Spirit can communicate with our soul, it means the moment we become saved our mind will be fully renewed as well.

But when you get born-again, your spirit gets renewed but your mind is exactly as dead as it has always been. And you have to go through a process the Bible calls the renewing of your mind, in Romans 12:2.

Romans 12:2 – *"And be not conformed to this world: but be ye transformed by the renewing of your mind, that ye may prove what is that good, and acceptable, and perfect, will of God."*

If the Spirit can communicate with our soul, it means by the time it touches our soul, our soul will be renewed instantly as well. But our soul is something we work on continually till Jesus comes.

You and I know that. The point is that the Holy Spirit always communicates with our spirit. It is now whether our spirit is able to then transmit that information to our soul, and our soul able to translate the information.

For instance, why is it when you are around certain people, a word of knowledge comes from them about what is happening in your life? How can you explain what happened? In this example, the person's intuition picked up a signal from the Spirit of God and that intuition translated that information to his mind and his mind was able to interpret that information and give it to you.

This is why many of us do not walk in the gifts of the Spirit even though we are praying for it. Usually the problem is not with our spirit communicating with the Spirit of God; that side is not the problem. The problem is our mind being able to receive that information and interpret it.

Evidence of communion in the Bible.

John 4:23 - *"But an hour is coming, and now is, when the true worshipers will worship the Father in spirit and truth; for such people the Father seeks to be His worshipers."*

Romans 8:16 – *"The Spirit Himself bears witness with our spirit that we are children of God".*

Romans 1:9 – *"For God, whom I serve in my spirit in the preaching of the gospel of His Son, is my witness as to how unceasingly I make mention of you…"*

1Corinthians 6:17 (AMP) – *"But the person who is united to the Lord becomes one spirit with Him."*

Sometimes the word communion is used for the words, serve, sing, united. It also means fellowship.

Those are the three functions of the human spirit. These 3 functions or elements of the human spirit function in a coordinated fashion.

Your conscience judges right from wrong but not based on stored knowledge because it is not the mind. Your conscience judges right from wrong based on intuition. So, intuition is what conscience relates to, in order to determine right or wrong. Just like the Spirit bears witness with your spirit that you are a son of God. A very good example I would like to give is smoking. You never find anywhere in the Bible where it says that smoking is a sin.

Don't go around preaching it. But we know the Bible says that our body is the temple of the Holy Spirit. If your body is the temple, do you then destroy that temple deliberately? Hence when many people still smoke after they get saved, that doesn't mean they are not saved.

You find that after a while they suddenly stop smoking. If you ask them why; they will say, something in their spirit just said, enough is enough. What happened there?

It is not you telling them to stop. They stopped because their conscience began to worry them about it based on intuition. Intuition picked up the signal from heaven saying ...stop smoking. And then intuition tells conscience and conscience says, stop smoking. Intuition sometimes is like a nagging child; it just wound not go away, until you yield. Sometimes, intuition is like that, it nags you. Stop smoking, stop smoking.

And it gets to a point where you just can't ignore it. This voice is a gentle voice, it is not a voice that slaps you around, it is a gentle voice. Conscience judges according to intuition. Intuition is related to communion or worship in that God is known by man intuitively. Let me put it this way – the human mind does not have the capacity to know God talk less of relating to God.

Think about it, if you are honest with yourself, sometimes you wake up and ask yourself, is there a God? Sometimes you see something and you ask, is there a God? Sometimes your mind becomes so blown away that it does not have the capacity to contain the concept of God talk less of find Him. The only way we know God is in our spirit.

Intuitively, you know there is God. If someone says prove it, you can't prove it. But you know. That kind of knowing is a spirit knowing, not a mind knowing. Because mind knowing tends to be able to be proven but spirit knowing is just known, period.

If somebody says are you saved? And how do you know? There is nothing you can say to defend that except to say that you just know. It is important for you to understand therefore that

God can only be known in our spirit and not in our mind.

The problem many believers have is that when we get saved, we have forgotten the fact that we need to develop the human spirit to be able to effectively relate with the Spirit of God. That is why the Bible says that strong meat is for those who by reason of use have their senses exercised. That is has a spirit and soul component.

Our spirit has a real function in our ability to be able to relate with God. In terms of our ability to relate with God with our spirit; it is not difficult, in fact in most cases it is automatic. The Spirit of God just does it; but the real battle ground is our mind.

Let me put it this way, if God wants to talk to you; He talks to your human spirit, your spirit relays it to your mind then your mind makes you aware of it, by interpreting it and bringing recognition.

If you have a mind that is polluted and renewed, always short-circuiting the flow, you find that whenever God speaks, everything is always ending in your human spirit; it is never relayed to your soul.

If you continue with that for a long time, you come to a point where you desensitise your soul completely, the ability to pick up signals from God becomes weaker and weaker and once that happens you become a slave to the flesh. It is important you understand this.

There is no way you can be a spiritually sensitive child of God, yet sin and not know it. It is not possible. There is no way you can sin and you tell me that you are not aware of it. If you are not aware of it knowledge wise, your conscience will tell you it is wrong by intuition.

That is the job of the conscience. Even when you don't know scripturally that it is wrong, if you are sensitive, your conscience will still tell you because your conscience is not a product of your knowledge. Its ability to tell you right from wrong has nothing to do with how much you know, it is purely a direct input from the Spirit of God.

Finally, I have added this segment as a BONUS Material to assist you in developing a healthy mind that will make hearing and obeying God easier.

A more detailed study of how the mind work is contained in one of my previous Books titled:

"Wrong Thoughts, wrong emotion and wrong living."

God bless you as you Obey Him and access His secret code to abundance, through Obedience which is a fruit of your righteousness in Christ Jesus.

Go and shine in the midst of your enemies. God bless you richly. It is a new day in your life and Jesus is Lord.

Books by Dr Charles Omole

1. *Church, Its time to Fly -- Learning to fly on Eagles Wing.*

2. *How to Avoid Getting Hurt in Church -- 13 Steps that will protect you and help create an atmosphere for breakthroughs.*

3. *Must I go to Church -- 8 Reasons why you must attend Church.*

4. *Freedom from Condemnation -- Breaking free from the burden & weight of sin.*

5. *I cannot serve a big God and remain small*

6. *How to start your own business*

7. *How to Make Godly Decisions*

8. *How to avoid financial collapse*

9. *Let Brotherly love continue: An insight into love and companionship.*

10. *Breaking out of the debt trap*

11. *Common Causes of Unanswered Prayer.*

12. *How to Argue with God and Win -- Biblical strategies on getting God's attention for all your circumstances all of the time*

13. *Avoiding Power Failure-- How to generate spiritual power for daily success and victorious living.*

14. *How long should I continue to pray when I don't see an answer?*

15. *SUCCESS KILLERS: Seven Habits of Highly Ineffective Christians.*

16. *The Financial Resource Handbook – UK Edition*

17. *Divine Strategies for uncommon breakthroughs: Living in the Reality of the Supernatural:*

18. *Keys to Divine Success*

19. *Wrong Thoughts, Wrong Emotion and Wrong Living*

20. *Secrets of Biblical Wealth Transfer*

21. *Journey into Fulfilment*

22. *Prosperity Unleashed – A Definitive Guide to Biblical Economics*

23. *No More Debt – Volume 1*

24. *Understanding Dominion*

25. *Advancement*

26. *Getting the Story Straight*

27. *Overcoming when Overwhelmed*

28. *The Spiritual Fitness Plan*

29. *Spiritual and Practical Steps to Command Value*

30. *Breakthrough Strategies for Christians in the Marketplace*

31. *Spiritual Keys to Financial Reward*

32. *The 7Ms of Marriage*

33. *Marketplace Leadership Capsule*

34. *Financial Intelligence for Christians in the Marketplace*

35. *Supporting Good Governance in the Nigerian Police – Vol 1*

For more information about our ministry, world outreaches and a free catalogue of our media and study materials, please write to:

Wisdom for Winning International
151 Mackenzie Road
London. N7 8NF,
UNITED KINGDOM

www.wisdomforwinning.org

Breakthrough Strategies for Christians in the Marketplace

CHARLES OMOLE

Author: Prosperity UnLeashed

BREAKTHROUGH STRATEGIES

FOR CHRISTIANS IN THE

Marketplace

Biblical Guide to the Strategic Invasion &
Reclaim of the Marketplace

The Marketplace is a spiritual entity; and money flows in the direction of spiritual power, either Godly or Satanic. Only those that are strong in God will be able to dislodge the economic system of Babylon. The final Battle for souls have begun....

FINANCIAL INTELLIGENCE
—— FOR ——
CHRISTIANS
IN THE
MARKETPLACE

Understanding Money Management, Debt, the Credit System and how to avoid the trap of the World's financial Order

CHARLES OMOLE LLB, LLM, PHD
AUTHOR: PROSPERITY UNLEASHED

Spiritual and Practical Steps to Command Value

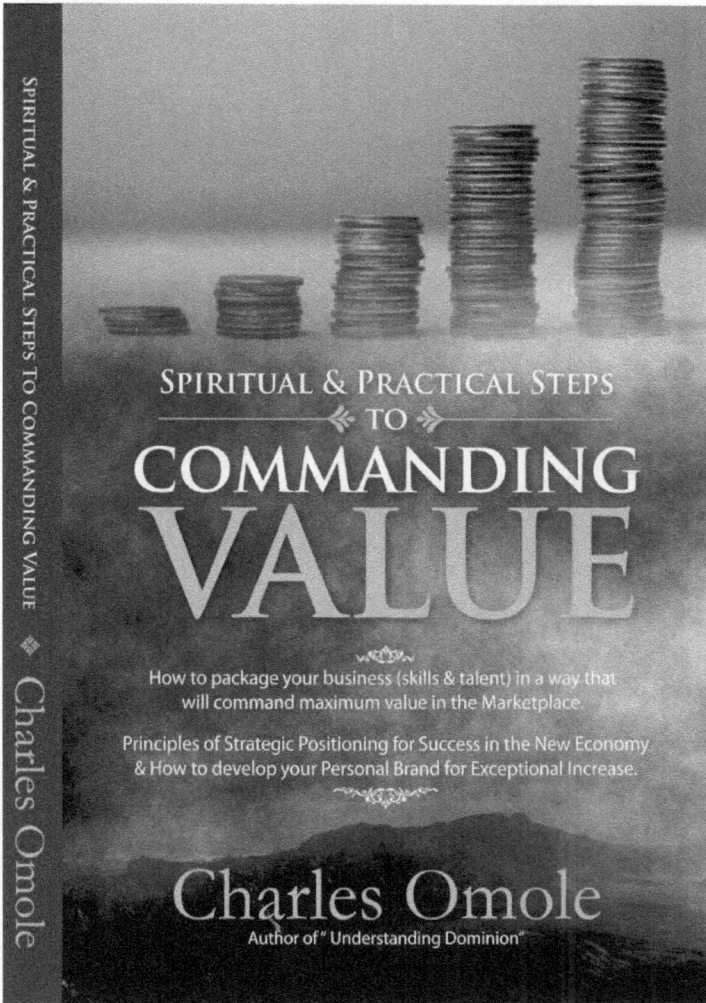

SPIRITUAL & PRACTICAL STEPS
— TO —
COMMANDING
VALUE

How to package your business (skills & talent) in a way that
will command maximum value in the Marketplace.

Principles of Strategic Positioning for Success in the New Economy
& How to develop your Personal Brand for Exceptional Increase.

Charles Omole
Author of "Understanding Dominion"

Spiritual Keys to Financial Reward

YOUR NOTES

YOUR NOTES

<u>YOUR NOTES</u>

<u>YOUR NOTES</u>

<u>YOUR NOTES</u>

<u>YOUR NOTES</u>